T0064551

what
IS
"success"
?

clarify your purpose and
review your beliefs

Catherine Palin-Brinkworth

M.AppSci (Social Ecology)

BALBOA.PRESS
A DIVISION OF HAY HOUSE

Balboa Press books may be ordered through booksellers or by contacting:

Balboa Press
A Division of Hay House
1663 Liberty Drive
Bloomington, IN 47403
www.balboapress.com.au
AU TFN: 1 800 844 925 (Toll Free inside Australia)
AU Local: 0283 107 086 (+61 2 8310 7086 from outside Australia)

Because of the dynamic nature of the Internet, any web addresses or links contained in this book may have changed since publication and may no longer be valid. The views expressed in this work are solely those of the author and do not necessarily reflect the views of the publisher, and the publisher hereby disclaims any responsibility for them.

The author of this book does not dispense medical advice or prescribe the use of any technique as a form of treatment for physical, emotional, or medical problems without the advice of a physician, either directly or indirectly. The intent of the author is only to offer information of a general nature to help you in your quest for emotional and spiritual well-being. In the event you use any of the information in this book for yourself, which is your constitutional right, the author and the publisher assume no responsibility for your actions.

Any people depicted in stock imagery provided by Getty Images are models, and such images are being used for illustrative purposes only. Certain stock imagery © Getty Images.

Print information available on the last page.

ISBN: 978-1-5043-2420-5 (sc)
ISBN: 978-1-5043-2421-2 (e)

Balboa Press rev. date: 01/22/2021

Dedication

This book is dedicated:

To those who have patiently or impatiently given me your love and support. You have given me courage strength and wisdom, and eventually the capacity to love myself. It is my intention to give the same to you.

Most especially it is dedicated to my magnificent son in whom I am well pleased. Perhaps my best teacher. Words cannot be found for the gift of him in my life.

To my extraordinary mentors, John Nevin, Paul Terry and Spike, all now serving in a different dimension. Thank you for the precious parts of your lives you shared with me, and for your wisdom.

And to you. The only pathway through my fears of inadequacy around being published was the thought of service to you. I dedicate my life-long learning to you, to passing on the philosophies and processes that have been enlightening for me. Thank you for allowing me to contribute to your life.

Contents

Introducing Catherine

...by John Nevin*

"Different things to different people.... That's what happiness is..."
So the song goes. This poses the question: could there be a direct
relationship between success and happiness?

Does one bring the other? And, if so, which comes first?

Before I wrote this introduction, I asked a number of successful people;
"What IS success?.... The answers were not too diverse. The following
sentence summed it up for most:

"Getting something or being someone that I'd hoped and planned for."

Now, that could be big money, or power, from one's work; it could
be a super relationship with one's family; or it could be becoming the
chief executive of a significant business. One thing's for sure, though;
success really is a personal thing. The world may judge you successful
or unsuccessful but only you know how successful you feel.

Top executives may look successful to the world but not to themselves if
they can't communicate with their kids. They must make that judgement
call in their lives. They must decide what they seek most.

Conversely, single working parents may consider themselves successful
for getting their kids through high school, even if they didn't get to a
management level in their work.

So many people need help redefining their own success. And I'm glad Catherine created this book.

Why? Because Catherine understands what success is – and why it's not the same thing for everybody.

Catherine has worked in corporations where she has had a direct input into creating success patterns for junior and senior executives. She has successfully led her own consulting and training business, and she has excelled as a professional speaker.

She is a fine mentor to many who seek success in their personal and professional lives.

Her articles in magazines have inspired scores of people to believe in their own success. I believe everyone wants to be successful but may need direction.

The pages of this book will not only help those seeking, but also those who are not consciously "in sync" with what they want. Success is about getting what you want. Happiness is about enjoying what you have.

So, success to you. I know you'll be happy when you get there.

John Nevin
Founder of SWAP Australia – Salespeople With A Purpose
Founder of Professional Speakers Australia, formerly National Speakers Association of Australia
Founder of Direct Selling Association of Australia

*John originally authored this introduction on this book's first edition. Although John has now passed, his work and his words live on. I am grateful for his family's permission to re-use it.

From the author

What IS success?

Why am I asking that question? Why do I beg you to ask it of yourselves? Is it that important? As many of us have learned during the horror of the Covid19 pandemic, it truly is.

It is part of our human nature to strive. To want more of what pleases us. And we will never find any satisfaction in achievement, if it's something we haven't clearly defined as what we want. Believe me.

First of all - if you are someone, like me, who always thought that whatever they did was not really that significant, or just not good enough, you need to identify what success is to you, so you'll know it when you get it.

Secondly, because too many of us strive too hard for someone else's goals. True for you? You'll know, if you use the word 'should' a lot. Should is always someone else's agenda.

Thirdly, because once you've got it, you might not want it – unless you've really thought it through. Be careful what you wish for.

Fourthly, and this is weird – perhaps you actually already have it, and you haven't realised it. Perhaps you have been beating yourself up for Not being a Success. And all the time you were.

We have learned over this last while, that what we assumed were our life goals and choices became less important compared to health and connection with our loved ones. We've learned to question our traditional definitions of Wealth. It's been an Interesting Time.

Please enjoy the read. Congratulate yourself continually. Make another commitment at the end of every section. Dip in and out to remind yourself of some very helpful principles.

And know that I'm wishing you every "success" that you see as possible, and many that I suspect you don't.

Catherine Palin-Brinkworth
M.App.Sci (Social Ecology) Dip. Couns.Psych.
Fellow, Institute of Managers and Leaders
Certified Speaking Professional – Global Speaking Fellow
catherine@progressperformance.com
www.catherinespeaks.com

1

WHAT IS 'SUCCESS'?

Your level of 'success' in this world is determined by how you see
yourself compared to who and what you have committed to be.
And guess who gets to make all the decisions and choices? Absolutely. It's all up to you!

Success.....success.....success....

Success, success, success – if you say it often enough you not only get tongue tied, you develop a lithp. If you hear it often enough, and think you are getting it rammed down your throat, you might develop a lot more than that. You might get bored, or jaded. Or worse. You might develop a sense of frightening inadequacy, a real fear of not measuring up, a deep concern about your own value. About whether or not YOU are a SUCCESS.

Actually, you might not develop at all.

I had a phone call from a man I had met at a conference where I had spoken. At that conference he was enthusiastic, confident, and proud of his achievements to date. In just the right frame of mind to go on to further fulfilment. The conference had been well run, he had been inspired by speakers, and fellow attendees. I remembered his positive mindset and his excitement about life to come.

However, during the telephone call only a few weeks later he told me that after the conference, he had gone back to his regional home base and had lost all of the motivation he'd gained, all of his courage and commitment to strive for more.

All he could think of was all the *real* achievers he had met - and he felt he didn't and couldn't measure up. He compared himself continually to what he had heard of their achievements. He used his own critical view of his own underperformance as his focus. So he became what he was afraid he might be: a non-performer. He just froze.

While we spoke, I discovered that he was a committed family man with a large brood of healthy grandchildren. And he was actually the developer of a wonderful program teaching language and communication skills to indigenous children in his area. Yet he still saw himself as a non-performer. Because he couldn't make the sales that others were making.

A while later I was speaking at a breakfast for a specialised group of successful women in business. Before my presentation we were 'networking' at my table, finding out about each other, and how we might support each other's work. I asked one older woman what her field of activity was. "Oh, I don't do anything, dear - I'm not a successful woman at all." Curious, I asked more questions. She told me she was 'just' the mother of one of the women present. She admitted she had three daughters. They were all healthy, well-educated and competent achievers in the world's eyes. I was shocked to realise that we have so defined success as to have this magnificent woman believe she had not done anything praiseworthy. Surely the raising of children into healthy adults is one of the most challenging tasks we can undertake? If you've done it, you'll know how demanding it is - and what a fantastic thing to accomplish!

One of the many things I've learned from all the experiences in my life, is that we can only ever live up to the level of belief we have in ourselves. It has become Catherine's First Law of Leadership.

It is an observable fact. If we believe, even for a smidgeon of a second, that we are capable of more and go for it, the results are amazing even to our own eyes. Just that flicker of belief will give us the courage and confidence to have a go – and we will achieve something, even if it's not the full outcome. We'll be closer to it than if we didn't start. Of course.

Whereas if we believe ourselves to be limited and incapable, the proof of that will automatically be shown to us. Because we will not even try – or if we do, it's half-heartedly. The resulting evidence will be overwhelming to us. Someone wise once said 'for those who believe no proof is necessary – for those who do not, no proof is enough'. It's true of all belief systems, and it's certainly true of our self-belief.

> **'.....If we believe ourselves to be limited and incapable, the proof of that will automatically be shown to us.'**

Guess how I know this? Because I have spent a large part of my life in self-doubt. From my biography on line, you can discover that I have achieved a fair bit in the world's eyes. I have explored this issue in many seminars and self-study. Yet still the doubt arises.

We all know that what we fear is what we attract, because our mind will always follow our most dominant thought, even if it's what we don't want. If you doubt me, just try *not* thinking of a pink elephant, right now. Ha hah – you thought of a blue one! But I bet the pink one is up in the corner.

And we also know that whatever we are focused on, we will see. In neuroscientific terms, whatever our attention is aroused by will alert a part of our brain called the Reticular Activating System – primarily responsible for sleep-wake transitions. By increasing blood flow for attention-driven activity, it enables our brain to register significance and to gallop into action to find it for us. For instance, when we decide to buy a certain model of car, suddenly we see them everywhere. So if we are focused on proving to ourselves that we can't do something – no problem. The proof will be right there in front of us.

Please believe me, I do know this from experience. And so do you. Later in this book, I will share with you some of my own journeys into and out of what I had defined as success. It's been a massively intrepid voyage of discovery; more terrifying and dangerous than I could have imagined. According to my words to you a few paragraphs back, it's been successful. Here's what I have learned:

There will always be people who are "better" than us. They may get better marks, earn more money, or have bigger houses or better cars, or they may seem to have a happier family life (and perhaps you'd be surprised). Sometimes they just seem to exude more confidence or motivation. (Like me). You tend to envy them, and think you could or should be more like them.

I've learned that comparisons can be poison. Terminal.

It doesn't hurt to have role models, examples of behaviours and lifestyles which fit our own ideal. That's often what provides inspiration, aspiration and encouragement. But the #1 Secret Ingredient is to identify your goals and priorities – you know that bit – it's not a secret at all! – AND then to stop there and double check.

First Check: Is that REALLY what you want? Will reaching those goals fit your existing values, will it give you what you want most in life with all the possible requirements and conditions? Are you sure it's not just a goal-set that's been socialised into you by your culture and community? Is it truly you? How do you know what your real values are? Look at your life. Your values are always in evidence. It's how your home has been created, how your time is prioritised, and what your relationships look like.

Double Check: If you still have unfulfilled goals and dreams – which most of us do - are you willing to do what you might need to do, be who you might need to be, experience what may arise, as you make the choices that will take you towards those goals? Are they all aligned – so for instance, you don't have to sacrifice a precious relationship in the quest for business growth – or at least so you are prepared for the negotiations and resolutions you might find yourself making. It's not about what's right or wrong, good or bad – it's about your choices, and what's true for you and your life. Get clear on what's negotiable and what's not, for you. Get clear on what really matters.

Here's the funny thing I've discovered. If you have a strong drive towards something enough to name it, and survive the double check, you actually have it somewhere in your life already. If you don't, it's an inescapable fact that it doesn't really matter to you. You only think it does. (Sorry).

> **'.....So envy and resentment are a waste of time and energy; it's ac-tion that will get you the result you want. '**

If it's already there – even in a tiny almost unrecognisable form, it's a matter of believing in yourself enough, and doing the things you know are necessary to nurture and grow. If you want to. You are loved already – and no amount of someone else's definition of success will bring you more love, or more self-belief. The only way forward is to be more of who you are.

So envy and resentment are a waste of

time and energy. It's Awareness, Alignment and Action that will get you the result you want.

But back to my friend at the conference. I think he had temporarily forgotten his ultimate lifetime goal – the only real, attainable and worthwhile goal I know: to use your potential to live up to your own personal dreams. Not anyone else's! And if you set your objectives for yourself every day, ensuring they are always SMARTER (Catherine's Version of an Old Formula - Specific Measurable Aligned Realistic Time-Bound Exciting and Ritten-down!) and you move forward no matter how slowly in the direction of your dreams, you will achieve them. And you are a success.

Ralph Waldo Emerson wrote: "To laugh often and much; to win the respect of intelligent people and the affection of children; to earn the appreciation of honest critics and endure the betrayal of false friends; to appreciate beauty, to find the best in others, to leave the world a bit better, whether by a healthy child, a garden patch, or a redeemed social condition; to know even one life has breathed easier because you have lived. This is to have succeeded."

I like that a lot. And I like mine too. You are a success, because you're going for it. You're breathing. And you are important, perhaps in ways you haven't discovered yet.

The Real You

___

When you're giving a present to someone you care about, you often devote time, effort, energy - and money - to the wrapping. With anticipation half the pleasure, it's fun to create excitement and enthusiasm for the actual item before it's even been revealed.

Perhaps (reviving memories of my childhood on Christmas morning) we even try and guess the contents of the gift by the shape, the kind of wrapping and the level of attention to it.

And so it is with our own visual image and personal presentation, I think. It's not only a legal requirement that we clothe ourselves in most places, it's also a means of communication for us. By what we wear, we actually let people know all sorts of non-verbal messages whether we realise it or not. It's one of the easiest communication tools at our disposal, and some of us are very good at making the most of it. Possibly sometimes too much of it?

What if you were given a gift, wrapped with gleaming bright colours, with brilliantly contrived ribbons and bows and an aura of glamour and promise - and you opened it to find a mouldy, rotting potato?

Do you ever fear people may see you like this? Are you even a tiny bit afraid while you're working on your outer presentation, that your inner reality doesn't really match?

I'm amazed by how many people I meet - together, balanced, successful people - who confide to those they trust that they don't know who they really are. They just don't have the self-knowledge, self-awareness, self acceptance and therefore the self-confidence they deserve. Some of us have been conditioned since we were very small to be so many things to so many different people so that we can gain acceptance and approval - sometimes we're not sure if we really are all or any of those things.

The most important thing to do? For now, just accept it. And allow the Awareness to grow.

Just allow that lack of confidence. Respect and honour it as serving you. Whatever you do, don't criticise or beat up on yourself – that will only push your confidence down, even if it wasn't already!

'We are all the good things we admire about others....'

We are all of those wonderful things that people think we are. And many more besides. We are all the beliefs we hold, attitudes we take, values and opinions we espouse. We are all the good things we admire about others, even if it is only in a tiny measure of potential. That's called 'projection' – you can actually never admire a quality in another that does not exist within yourself, or you would not even be able to recognise it. You are all the generosity you have ever given, all the warmth that has made anyone smile, all the courage you have ever felt.

And we also have the potential to behave as badly as we sometimes see others doing.

But here's a riddle. There is one thing we are that everyone else is too, which makes us completely different to everyone else.

We are unique. One-off. I am, you are, so is he, and she. All different and all meant to be so.

That can be very tough.

Intellectually, we know and accept it; we've heard it often enough. But emotionally and behaviourally we sometimes rebel and deny it. Because we want to 'belong'.

I recall a prominent behavioural scientist describing his conversations with a group of young people, all protesting wildly that they want to be treated as individuals but all dressed in the same 'in' gear.

Who really wants to be different? Everyone ridicules people who are different! I want to be the same as…. I want to be regular, average, normal! Accepted!

I don't know about you, but I truly spent a large part of my younger life feeling and thinking like that. Trying to be ordinary, not to shine too brightly, not to threaten and alienate friends and family - classic fear of success stuff. I wanted to fit in, not stand out! Does any of this sound familiar to you? Even if you don't feel this way, do your kids?

Do you hamper your own brilliance through your reluctance to accept and develop your uniqueness? Please don't - we need you!

No other being in the entire universe, in the past, now, or in the years to come, can make the contribution you can make to your family, to your friendship circle, to your business, to this country and to the world. You are truly a worthy, worthwhile one-off person. I think that's why you were born.

You are actually a designer item. Please resist the temptation to become "mass-produced" - rare items are priceless. You're so special. In order to be irreplaceable, you have to be different.

'....in order to be irreplaceable you have to be different. '

The Real You is Magnificent.

Let everyone know, without saying a word. Remember the 3 V's – Visual, Vocal and Verbal communication. Use the first two to deliver the Real You.

You may be living with limited money to spend – at the moment. But healthy exercise – walking, swimming, cycling – may be accessible to you at very little cost, so getting your precious body into its best shape can usually be managed. If you're stuck here, it's almost always a symbol of being stuck elsewhere – often in rebellion or powerlessness. Trust me, I've lived it.

I had the gift of dance classes as a child. I'm grateful to be reminded in my head of 'shoulders back, tummy in, tail under' – thank you Miss Peters! Because when I claim my best posture, suddenly I look and act like I value my own magnificence. Interesting, really – there goes that Alignment word again.

Clothing can be so inexpensive, if we hunt around. I clothed myself and my son from charity shops while I was growing my business, and was continually complimented. We can do 'swaps' with friends, we can make an old garment look better in all sorts of ways. There are far greater experts than I am on image and styling on a budget – try the search engines. Here's the point. It does matter what you wear and how you wear it, because of the visual messages you are conveying. Not to cover up or disguise who you are, but to display it. Because you ARE magnificent. So wear it, stand it, move it.

When you speak with people, do they hear – and want to hear more – from the Real You?

When I coach senior executives in presentation skills I love digging deep and finding out who they really are, the real stories that have shaped their lives. Once we find that magnificence, it's easy to work with it.

So I'd love you to re-discover the magnificence you may have forgotten or taken for granted. Please – I'm not telling you to tell anyone about it! I just want you to know it. Because with that quiet relaxed inner knowing, you will be way more able to seek out the magnificence in the people you are talking with, whether professionally and personally. And when they know you can see it, without a word, they will relax, be real with you, and form trusting relationships. That makes all success so much easier.

Do you share your thoughts clearly with intended respect for others, making your communication style part of your gift wrapping? Do you respect your own messages enough to learn how to deliver them at your best? Not with any fake, mechanical, insincere 'presentation skills' that you might be taught at classes or clubs. But with a genuine expression of your own heart, for a clear purpose and for the benefit and wellbeing of others.

Most success paths need good communication skills, whether written or spoken. And there hasn't been a baby born, as far as I know, who already has them. They are always learned. Some folks might seem to do it more easily than others. Be careful. Everything is a gift. And every strength taken to an extreme can become a liability.

And the other communication method – that which Carl Jung called 'the collective unconscious' – the unexpressed inner thoughts and feelings that others can read, is arguably the most important of all. It's your inner knowing. Do you know you already ARE a success? Just thought I'd remind you!

Who are you trying to please?

"When I hear a man applauded by the mob, I always feel a pang of pity for him. All he has to do to be hissed is to live long enough".

H L Mencken

While studying Change Consultancy with the inimitable Scott Washington a few years back, I discovered that babies are born with two fundamental emotional needs – Validation (you're OK, you are a valid human being and you matter) and Nurturing (it's OK, you will be looked after.) In my experience, we never lose those two needs. When they're met, you'll be having a happy healthy life. When they're not, you will have pain.

So we spend our lives looking for people who will meet both those needs and when we find them, we tend to stay with them for as long as they keep it up.

Sometimes we don't find them easily. Perhaps in our childhood we were not validated or nurtured – or both – so the belief is formed unconsciously that we do not deserve to be honoured and cared for. If that's so, and it is for a lot of us, we will actually push people away who will honour and care for us, because it just doesn't fit our sense of 'normality'. We may not be conscious of doing that, but look at your life, and see if it's so.

Maybe we have felt a bit unloved and unappreciated in an area of our life. Maybe in many areas. Look at homeless people in the streets or parks and you'll see it.

And so we spend the most unbelievable amount of time, energy and effort, and sometimes money, trying to please others so we will get the Validation and Nurturing we want.

We need approval (we think!). We crave the smile of acceptance, the warm eye contact, the friendly touch, the better job, the increased pay packet, more customers or clients etc. Why? Because it means we're wanted, needed and appreciated. And perhaps others will admire us.

At the other end of the spectrum, we live in fear of not being found pleasing. Every manager who critiques our performance, every customer who doesn't want our services is rejecting us personally. Every refused offer or invitation is an icy rejection, causing shivers of hurt, and a cold inner fear of inadequacy. Am I exaggerating? What do you think?

I've been there. Not so much when selling or marketing someone else's product or services – because that was always done with a focus on commitment to the client's wellbeing, and it wasn't about me.

> ' .... most of us spend the most unbelievable amount of time, energy and nerve power, just trying to please. '

But if you've ever had to market yourself, as a coach, consultant, speaker, trainer, adviser, etc. (or life partner!) you may have a feel for how scary it is when YOU are the product that may be rejected, as well as the seller of it!

(Don't worry, I survived – even thrived – and I'll share how.)

Needing to please, in any environment, can be very stressful. It's just not an easy and comfortable way to live. Even if you don't feel stressed by it, there will be some fear/hurt/pain suppressed somewhere, and that can do even more damage than visible stress symptoms.

Maybe that's OK. There's a lot of research material available on the optimal levels of stress needed for peak performance. Not just in business, but in sport and in home and family life. It's called 'eustress'. It could be called 'being kept on your toes". Most of us know that if we're pushed too far, though, or it goes on for too long, it turns our stress into distress, and our performance fades as we cross over that excess of stress. What causes that distress?

In many cases it's that desperate, compulsive need for approval. The lack of a strong, clear, confident identity independent of others' views.

Here are a few examples of the self-defeating beliefs and attitudes that arise in that situation:

"I need to be loved or approved of by people in my life - and if I'm not, I'm worthless", or
"I must not fail or make errors, if I do, it's terrible", and even
"People and events should always be the way I want them to be".

Here are some more rational achievement statements –
"It's definitely nice to have people's love and approval - but even without it, I can still accept and enjoy myself", and

"Doing things well is satisfying - but it's human to make mistakes", and of course
"People are going to act the way they want - not the way I want".

'....others do not exist to please us – nor we them.... '

Once we come to terms with the reality that others do not exist to please us - nor we them - but rather learn to relate and interact in an adult objective manner, our relationships become more settled and relaxed.

A mentor shared with me some guidance he had been given: "Beware when all speak well of thee". It's proven to be good counsel. Those who depend too heavily on the positive acceptance of all around them soon learn the pain of the swinging pendulum. It's a very risky dependence.

Just be you. It IS good enough. In fact, it's magnificent.

Please your customers with good service, your employer or colleagues with honest commitment to agreed objectives, and your family and friends with the love and respect you give them. In accordance with your own values and boundaries, your own life principles, your true and authentic presence. Because when you're at your best, there's no one better at being you. You ARE a success.

Look at what you've got!

A business associate and I were sitting talking about the development of his business - in particular, the extension of his product range. As we talked - and listened - to each other, a lot of fairly vital common sense started to emerge. Have you ever had that happen to you?

You think you are discussing one topic and suddenly you realise you are actually uncovering another, and it is something so basic, yet so important, it influences not only the outcome of the current discussion but also a number of other decisions you will make in the future.

What my friend and I had been discussing was a research project designed to uncover and clearly define the "culture" or personality of an organisation. Not necessarily in flattering terms, but to try to see the organisation as others outside it see it.

The next step was NOT to decide whether to change it or not. It seemed logical that it had taken that organisation some time to develop that personality and to try to alter it was going against the proven evolutionary trend. It is a very successful organisation, in its own way, in its own style and in the words of that great old maxim, if you're on to a good thing, stick to it! So the next step was to develop products and service methods to capitalise on that personality which would identify with it in harmony, using its strengths.

For many of you, this will seem like a pretty simple explanation of a basic marketing exercise. But did you ever stop and realise how much all this common sense business practice translates so cleverly to your own personality, your own potential? You, Yourself, Personally, Inc? Or Me Pty Ltd?

Well, I tell you, I just sat down after my associate had left, and did the whole thing all over again on Me just for the fun of it!

There is little point in undergoing this analysis for the sake of a bit of good old-fashioned self-flagellation. It is very easy to find the things that are wrong with you; if you ask around, most people are happy to tell you. Many do even if you don't ask them!

But the very things that you think are wrong with you (or your company, or your product range, or even your community) may well be the things that make you (or your company, etc) as strong as you are in other areas.

For instance, someone told me the other day that he had once been described as blunt and critical. That's true, he is. Those behavioural characteristics are an outcome of a very frank, open, analytical and out-spoken personality. He is a joy to do business with. He does not play games, he tells it as he sees it, and his so-called blunt and critical nature is one of his greatest personal selling points. He does usually deliver his messages with politeness and some sensitivity!

I was involved in a group seminar once where we were encouraged to share with our co-participants something we didn't like about them. Ugh! Pretty heavy! And not an exercise I would encourage. I chortled

Catherine Palin-Brinkworth

when the accusation levelled at me was with regard to a characteristic I have consciously and deliberately developed for some time. You can't win them all, I guess.

But think about this. If you can't do a good job being who you are, you're going to find it rather more difficult being who you are not.

Look at what you've got and use it. Build on it. Whether you are reading this and relating it to your company, your range of goods and services, yourself, or any other facet of your life, work out what your strengths are, and expose them to the world. We've talked about communicating the real you. So this is about getting clear on the hugely valuable components of the Real You.

> *'....Look at what you've got and use it.'*

Whatever they may be, they took some time getting there and a lot of effort probably went in to their creation and development. In business, we list our establishment costs, and the goodwill resulting from our service to customers, as an asset. In life, we need to do the same. All of the effort you have put into your strengths, your capabilities, your education, your experience – especially in the hard times – are your greatest gifts. I guarantee you that the more difficult your life has been, the more hurdling skills you have developed, the more value you are in this world.

You ARE magnificent. You cannot not be. Your focus now is on using that magnificence in the most magnificent way; claiming the future you know you can create. Whatever anyone else thinks of it doesn't matter.

I have laughed with my son about my early dreams for him to be a plastic surgeon – for the obvious reasons! More seriously, as he grew I imagined him as a clean cut conservative young man, straight out of a few style magazines. He's not. He is intensely creative, free-wheeling, and distinctly himself. He's passionate about what he does, is hugely successful, and I couldn't be prouder of him. Most particularly, I honour his honesty, his authenticity and his kindness. How he looks and what he does for a living are completely irrelevant, they fade into the background behind those shining values. Who he is, is a gift to this planet, and to his partner and child. And so are you. Look at what you've got.

As a fabulous young person once said to me: "Wanting to be like somebody else is wasting the person you already are".

Your quest for Success will hopefully never stop. Even if we are struggling in our final years to feed ourselves – we will keep trying when we are encouraged.

Whatever you want in your life now, approach it with gratitude for all you have already accomplished - even if you don't think it's much. Do a thorough inventory of your gifts and blessings. That's the only way Success will get easier for you. When you remember how far you've already come and encourage yourself to expand just a little further.

You have everything it takes to reach your goals and dreams, or you would not have them. Just take it off the shelf, give your beliefs a good scrub and polish, and head on out. Success is waiting for you.

'...remember how far you've already come and encourage yourself to expand just a little further.'

21

Sorry. It's ALL up to you

E very now and again it comes to me again how different everyone is.

It's so easy when you're working in management, in service, in sales or marketing to target and classify people in terms of their group behaviour. Well, maybe not always easy, but we do it anyway. And of course, we have to, or our tasks would be unworkable and unmanageable.

But in microvision, when we stand at street level and really look at ourselves and those around us, we are all incredibly different.

I had quite a heated argument once with a Scotsman in a bar in Vail, Colorado (yes, the skiing was lovely, thank you). I mention the location only to convey the exotic atmosphere and the possible distortion of logic. He maintained steadfastly, from a global marketing point of view, that human beings were not unique. He argued that all our behaviour is en masse and is continuously capable of being recognised and predicted that way.

You may believe that too, and I could be running the risk of another heated argument here. But to me, we are all the product of our own thought patterns, which are undeniably unique, although from time to time common stimuli may provoke common reactions.

So, if you'll ride with me for now, and agree that we are all different, it's great fun to think through the amount of control we all have over everything that happens to us, or at very least in the way we respond to it.

It's actually why siblings, even identical twins, can end up with very different lifestyles and outcomes, from the same environment and genetics. And it's exciting.

Life is our choice. Everything. Every situation is one of cause and effect, action and reaction. If we don't believe we can cause our circumstances, we know we can certainly control our response to them. That's an enormous awareness to grasp. It gradually hits you at a number of levels, doesn't it? Quite matter-of-factly on the surface, but oh-my-gosh when you really start applying it to today's events and tomorrow's and beyond. And it never stops hitting you, if you're open to it.

How often do you here people say, "He made me do it"? How often have you said, "She makes me so mad!"? How often have we adopted a point of view because of its popularity?

Here's the way it is. No one can ever make us do, feel or think anything. We always have the choice. We simply need to understand the consequences and we make our decisions. Our lives truly are our own. And we get to live them.

It's so easy for us to deny responsibility, to lay the blame elsewhere if it goes wrong and often out of trained modesty to give away the credit when it goes really well! Both of those are crazy! Surely the answer to either scenario is "Thank you!" For the learning, or for the compliment. They're both valuable.

I was given a plaque as a speaker gift once, and I really like the inscription:

"The difference between a successful person and others is not a lack of strength, not a lack of knowledge, but rather in a lack of will."

It's from Vince Lombardi, a renowned American football coach. He ranks first among NFL coaches by total championships won. He was known for his determination to win.

As a leader of several teams in my life, I know how frustrating it is to see talent and capability and see it unfulfilled. We see it often; people trained, motivated, inspired, coached and helped who still do not perform to their potential. It's because they have to choose to succeed, themselves, setting their own burning personal objectives. It has to be their will, and their own self-acknowledged responsibility.

Over the last decade, another dimension to success has projected itself onto the movie screen of my mind. Belief. Without it, all the will in the world won't work, and the talents and abilities are wasted.

I have to be real with you, and tell you that for quite a while, I wanted to be rescued. When I was raising my son alone, when my business faltered occasionally, when my health failed completely – I so longed for the white knight on the shining horse – or any horse really – to come and take care of it all for me.

Surprise! It didn't exactly work out that way. But eventually, I realised it was my responsibility to deal with what was happening and to get on with it. And so it is with all of us.

Not trying to please others, not concerned with what friends and colleagues will think of us. But after a weighing up of choices and consequences, making a decisive commitment to a course of action and a set objective – and going for it. Being prepared to do whatever it takes to get there - after weighing up the alternatives and side effects. And learning to negotiate with the other people in our lives, so we have people fighting for us, not against us.

I don't think Lombardi was talking about willpower, by the way. There's a difference between willpower and will. Willpower implies to me that I have to push through with determined effort, that it will be hard, that I have to overcome every obstacle, and never never never give in. That might be necessary at times. But a life lived entirely through willpower is exhausting and potentially destructive. It seems to be devoid of any response to feedback, and to lack in the search for self-awareness.

I'm talking will as in choice. I get to choose. Sometimes the choice is obvious, according to our values or goals. And sometimes it's not — when a decision either way could work.

'....there are no shoulds. They are always someone else's agenda. '

It's not about 'shoulds' either. I simply don't believe in them, and I won't have them in my life. They are always someone else's agenda. There are choices I could make, there are decisions that either align with my goals and values or not. But there are no shoulds.

I brought my boy up on choices and consequences. I remember him stamping his foot at about six, saying "I'm sick of choices!" I could only sympathise, and assure him there were plenty more coming.

For anyone who needs a guarantee of safety or approval, who needs to believe that there is a right way so they can do it, this is difficult to accept sometimes. It might seem easier to have a rigid set of rules with pre-destined consequences. And that's another choice. My belief system, my faith, tells me that I am loved whatever choice I make. Each choice will have a consequence, from which I can learn and grow, or benefit hugely (I like those ones) or fall into a pit and weep (which I have done at times).

Shakespeare wrote "To thine own self be true."

It really is up to you. It's your life. Don't let anyone else live it for you. Live it your way, love your freedom and authority, and celebrate your decisions. You can always make another one if you don't like the results. As the wonderful speaker Jim Rohn said "If you don't like it, move! You're not a tree."

That's success.

It's always the right time

Are you ever guilty of procrastination? Or think you are?

Throughout my life, I have whipped myself into paralysis with self-criticism and negative judgement. I'm often seen by others as a high achiever – but in my own mind for many years, all I saw was what I hadn't done, rather than what I had. And I knew I was a shocking procrastinator.

Well, right now, I am sitting here laughing as I write this. That was so ridiculous!

'.....I've discovered how perfect procrastination really is.'

Because I've discovered how perfect procrastination really is.

If it needed to be done – like cooking, eating, sleeping, walking, looking after my family and the most pressing of my clients – I did it. And if it was optional (often sounding like a 'should') I often didn't.

My father, whose sense of humour was totally unique, used to say "Never put off till tomorrow what you can do the day after." I heard it, and I made it my own. Of course I met deadlines – for clients and colleagues, for my family, for my university assignments – but mostly at the last minute. The self-inflicted whip marks on my back grew deeper and thicker.

Until one day when I discovered an amazing tool called Instinctive Drives. For the first time, I realised that my Gift, my innate success drive, is to Improvise. To Beat the Odds. It wasn't anything to be ashamed of or guilty about – even though our society would like everyone to comply with a more structured work approach – it was and is my best way of working. I have so much more energy and creativity at the 11th hour than I ever could at the 2nd or 3rd hour. It's the way I'm wired, and it works. You could also check out the Kolbe Conative Index; I believe it's from the same original research base.

Some time later, when undertaking certification in the Myers Briggs Type Indicator, which is committed to making the theory of psychological types described by C. G. Jung understandable and useful in people's lives, I discovered that I have a Perceiving preference vs Judging. (I'm an ENFP, in case you're curious). This is NOT about being perceptive or judgemental. It is more about whether you prefer a more structured and decided lifestyle (Judging) or a more flexible and adaptable lifestyle (Perceiving).

To others, I seem to prefer a flexible and spontaneous way of life, and I like to understand and adapt to the world rather than organize it. People see me staying open to new experiences and information. So of course I have to put everything off until the last minute, in case there are some more ideas I can include!

If my preference was Judging, I would seem to prefer a planned or orderly way of life, liking to have things settled and organized, and feel more comfortable when decisions are made. I'd want to bring life under control as much as possible.

So it's all good. Once again, it is about discovering and delighting in difference. So to all my J friends whom I have driven crazy over the years, thank you for hanging in. And to my P friends – hey, we're OK!!

Why do I share this? Because we are always all we ever need to be. The differences you have criticised yourself for, are your gifts. Your unique way of being. The only way you become joyful, enriched, successful, is by living you.

Back on the topic of time, I now know that everything always happens exactly when it will be of the most value to you. You may not always like that. Life is not designed to make us happy or comfortable. It is designed to make us strong, if we have the courage and commitment to go through our difficulties without complaining and falling into victimhood.

It seems to me that some of us have developed an addiction to comfort, unlike earlier generations who were more stoic and expected little from life. None of that is bad or wrong. But it does help us understand why we find life challenging.

I'm very sure that everyone reading this book will have gone through the year of 2020, and will have experienced the challenges that year brought us. Some have been horrific, and completely life changing. Some have been difficult but manageable. Every challenge has brought us a gift in some way, perhaps learning how little we actually need for survival, how much our loved ones mean to us and how our values have shifted in priority.

'Every challenge has broughtus a gift in some way....'

In Australia our year began with uncontrollable bush fires – or wildfires – where whole towns were destroyed and lives lost. We wept for the losses of so much, and we donated all we could for those impacted. And as the heat of our southern summer passed, we discovered Covid19.

As an island continent, we have the seas and oceans for borders and protection. But a cruise liner brought the virus and air travellers accelerated the spread. So we have learned about the importance of distance, of changes to habits and to the 'rights' we took for granted. We have learned to value time, because in fact it is the only certainty in our lives. And our 'hurry-worry' has diminished. Because our former achievement goals no longer seem as important as simply living, loving and laughing when we can.

Have you ever encountered an old proverb that says "Procrastination is the Thief of Time"?

Personally, I have never seen anything steal time as cleverly as ill health. It is no stranger to me, and I have lost years to it. Did I have a choice? Several, but they were not all consciously available to me at the time. Do I resent that stealth? I have, in the past. I remember one of John Nevin's favourite sayings : "Anger and resentment are acids that corrode the vessel holding them." So my life will not be improved by resisting and resenting what is. Best give thanks for the silver linings, even if we can not yet see them, and accept that everything in time is valuable.

My old teacher, Spike, taught me impermanence. Everything is impermanent. Good feelings, bad feelings, grief, frustration, and happiness. All will pass. My best strategy is to not hold on to them. To relax and allow. To make the most of every moment. To be thankful, even when I don't like what's happening. This too shall pass.

So back to procrastination.

Do you have an ironing basket? I know that some people actually like ironing, and many wonderful people do it for their living. Me? I'm bad. My ironing basket is nearly always full, and only gets attention at the last minute (of course). Perhaps I'm waiting for an Ironing Angel to knock on my door – or some other wonderful dream to come true. Yes, I know I could buy non-iron clothes – but I love to wear linen and cotton in our climate and ….you know.

So I have developed the CPB Ironing Basket Theory of Life.

If you want to wear it, take it out of the basket and iron it. If you don't, leave it there. Every six months, whatever is in the basket goes to a Refuge or someone who needs my clothes. Yes, it's an incentive for me to iron, if I want to keep the garments. But more importantly, it's common sense. If I don't want to wear it, why spend the time ironing it?

Where's the Theory of Life? If I want to do something, I will do it. Often not because I like the doing, but because I want the result. If I don't want to do it, nor want the result, I won't do it. Give the 'shoulds' away. Give the tasks away. They do not bring me joy. They are not the best use of my time.

This may or may not bring me the kind of life I once thought I wanted to live. But now, I want to live with joy, celebrating the hours days months and years that are the gifts of time. Choosing how I can be of the most service and value to the world, and claiming that value. That is how I see time. An investment in my happiness, or my strength. Misery is The Thief of Time, and I don't have time for it.

2

THE WAY WE ARE – UNTIL WE'RE NOT

For all onward progress, some of what is necessary is facing 'reality'. Accepting the concept of self-determination. Understanding our limitations (if we choose to) and our needs, developing a good positive working knowledge of our own resources. That all helps to ensure we build our own success on today's ground, with confidence in our capacity to fulfil our dreams. We need to face a few facts, perhaps take a bit of advice, and then go for it.

War & Peace

On't be daunted by the title – this is not a major epic. It is, however, a comment on something I feel extremely strongly about: War In Our Worlds.

No, not in other parts of our planet. Not in other people's worlds. In Our Worlds.

It's one of the most destructive conditions in any part of our lives. Everyone suffers. Whether it's our work colleagues, our families and friends, our customers, suppliers and shareholders. Or our governments. It wastes time and resources, it breaks people and relationships, and it rarely provides any value.

It came to mind with some force when I was invited to address a youth convention on the topic of Peace.

It was Anzac Day, actually, and it felt good. That is the annual commemoration of the day the Anzac forces from Australia and New Zealand landed in Turkey at Gallipoli on April 25, 1915 to hideous slaughter and incredible heroism. It is a sacred day, to remember the courage and commitment of the fallen in all wars and to celebrate peace.

The youth convention was wonderful, the young attendees even more so, and as I prepared my presentation and then delivered it, the importance of what I was saying became obvious to me – it was not just about political war of course, but about life in general, and it specifically resonated with me around workplaces I knew, where we spend so much of our lives, and around families.

The discussion that followed was also not so much about world peace, a topic vital to our growing generation, but about personal peace – because you can't have one without the other.

We talked about the real acceptance of oneself, and of our fellow earth-walkers. We addressed questions around the causes of anger, hate and deliberate destruction – the very human factors of fear, greed and ignorance. We worked out some techniques for cutting destructive thoughts and wishes as they arose and using our precious time and energy for achievement instead.

They say you teach most what you need to learn. And as we worked through it all I related it to my own business world, and to past experiences in my family.

Why are so many people at war with each other? We see the massive problems of road rage in our so-called civilisations, the gang wars in our cities, and the school shootings in the United States of America. I see businesses and organisations at war with their suppliers and even their clients! I hear so much from employees at war with their employers, their managers, their colleagues. How many leaders seem to spend their lives under attack from their teams? How many employees nurture anger and resentment about systems, errors, or perceived inadequacies? I hear it in workshops and in coaching sessions!

And families are so often a similar battleground. It's exhausting.

If war is being waged at management or directorial level, what hope does a business have of providing valuable customer service and positive benefits to the market place? All under the pressure of providing a profitable return on investment to the shareholders.

It would seem to me to be impossible to get excited about providing a service and explaining its benefits, or to convince anyone of the desirability of becoming a client, if we are angry or dissatisfied. From my point of view, it is the first and most vital requirement for an employee, whatever his or her role, to be absolutely committed to the benefits the business can offer. Complete enthusiasm, even to the degree of a burning sense of mission, is essential to success. Research shows that only 15% of us really claim we love our work. The rest of us would rather be doing something else. It's pretty had to become a top performer at something you would rather not be doing.

'....complete enthusiasm, to the degree of a burning sense of mission, is essential to success.'

When we are part of a family we don't enjoy being around (it happens) or hanging around with a bunch of friends who don't inspire us – why? We can actually move! As I've shared elsewhere, the late great Jim Rohn would say "If you don't like being where you are, move. You're not a tree!"

Maybe it's a good idea to re-examine why you're doing what you're doing. Do you really believe in the benefits of your product/service/company? If you do, are there things about it that bug you to the extent of creating continuing anger or resentment? Would you be better off elsewhere?

If the people around you aren't aligned with your values and life principles, bless them and let them go! Don't ever let fear stop you from living a life of peace. That is insane.

So deal with the things you are waging an internal war over. Change them if you can, constructively and positively. Do anything you can to make an improvement if you really believe it would make a difference.

I've always loved anthropologist Margaret Mead's statement "Never doubt that a small group of committed determined people can change the world – indeed it is the only thing that ever has."

And if you need to, come to an acceptance and drop completely any past memories that take up expensive emotional and mental space. There's no room for baggage in most success journeys. Travel light.

Most importantly, be at peace. Somehow you get a lot more done that way.

It's not not fair

One of the most common cries we hear from those around us these days seems to be "It's not fair!" I heard it from my son when he was little. I've probably said it myself when I wasn't thinking. We've been fed the line since we were children - "It's not fair!" Somehow we have been led to believe that it should be fair. Well, guess what? It's NOT fair. And it's NOT not fair!

This is really important.

Imagine a world where everyone got the same. Regardless of their energy, effort, skill, commitment, determination. Where no matter how you were born or what your parents did for you or how hard you worked for yourself, you got exactly the same as everybody else. Is that fair? What do you think? You might be tempted to say "yes!'" because it would certainly absolve you of any responsibility – but it would also take away any incentive for you to make more of your life. You'd have no clear reason to use your talents and skills to their best form of service, and you'd eventually become robotic if not if not despairing.

But that's exactly what most of us are crying for when we say "It's not fair!"

I remember when a friend returned a few years back from working overseas in a determinedly egalitarian country, filled with horror that a specialist doctor who had studied for years was paid the same as a taxi driver, who was obviously skilful but not at the same level. That economy has since changed dramatically, the former version simply was not sustainable. Do you think we would really like 'fair' it if we had it? What is 'fair' anyway?

One of the most precious and exciting things about our lives is our freedom, which we probably grossly underestimate. Each one of us, regardless of our trade or profession, has total freedom to work and earn much, or not work and earn little; to serve our customers or employer or family, or not to. If we can't get a job somewhere, we can move somewhere else, or learn to do something else. Or start our own business. Our lifestyle is our own choice. That's awesome.

'....Our lifestyle is our own choice. '

The right to determine our own level of success and the degree of fulfilment of our own potential – what a privilege to cherish!

Those who would seek to have everyone aspire to the same lowest common denominator, to make it "fair", could look at the potential penalties for hard work and achievement that would impose, and the reward for minimum effort they would be granting. Of such ideals is mediocrity born.

Any sales manager who has ever taken a healthy territory from a top sales rep to give it to a struggler has played the "It's not fair" game. Any employer who has ever cut back an incentive program because the top performer got it every time and the bottom ones didn't, has played it too.

Every school sports day where every child wins a prize is playing it. Every birthday party where the siblings are given presents too because we can't leave them out, is in the midst of it.

Life was not meant to be fair. Nature is not fair.

Please don't get me wrong – over the centuries our man-made rules and laws have often been discriminatory and uncivilised. Even in my own lifetime, equal opportunities for anyone who wants to grow and succeed have been fought for and in many countries, won. In some countries, sadly not yet. And in our most supposedly civilised environments, some magnificent human beings still struggle to be considered and appreciated for their potential contribution rather than rejected for their size shape age colour or fitness.

'...Life was not meant to be fair. Nature is not fair.....'

The aim for a world of universal respect and decent treatment for all, is still to be strived for.

But in reality, some will always be more successful than others. It's the higher achievers who provide the inspiration and often the motivation to others to strive for more. Everyone's level of service is of value, and we are all on a path to greater and greater value - we need to know it's worth the effort. A goal to achieve, to succeed in what we believe is a worthy endeavour, is really crucial to our mental and emotional health. We need to know ourselves as capable of more, and experience the joy of reaching and succeeding.

Recently I've heard a lot of people talking about our rights. Our birthrights. Our human rights. This might upset you, or even make you angry. That's not my intention (and of course I can't make you angry, only you can.)

But I'm not sure who authored or initiated those rights. I think back to my son's birth, and although I was fairly exhausted at the time, I'm fairly sure no-one endowed him with any 'rights'. It honestly seems to me that the only right he had was to draw breath. Everything else was a privilege.

As a woman, reaching adulthood in discriminatory times, I am certainly passionate about being treated equally and given the same opportunities as a man would. You could say that would be fair. But only if the man were of equal talent and capability as me. In whose eyes? We are all subjective in our observation of others. We all have preferences, even filters that shape our perceptions differently. I remember being amazed when I studied physics that I could actually see colours differently to others, purely because of the way the light entered my eyes. That's right, brown isn't brown. It's millions of different hues and shades of brown depending on your amazing rods and cones!

So my determination to be non-discriminatory is admirable, and I want to continue that journey. It will be easier for me when I remember that there will always be differences and discriminations that I may or may not see, and that may or may not be a problem. I will do my very best to see people as individuals, all with differences, rather than stereotypes. However I may not always be fair in their eyes.

Do we have a right to free education, or free medical care for instance? (Hey, I'm really sorry, this is not meant to be a political commentary – and it won't be.) I love my country and the incredible support systems it provides. Is it always fair? No. We do our best. And the rest is mostly handled well by community commitment.

Success in my mind, for my values, includes positive supportive relationships. So when I do my best to treat people fairly (which does not mean tit for tat, or an eye for an eye) it goes towards success. Does that make sense? I also know I like to be treated politely and with respect. But I can't enforce that. I might like to think of it as a right. But the people who don't treat me with respect obviously don't agree with that. And no amount of insisting that it is my right, will make any difference.

Our rights have to be agreed to with the other people involved, or they don't exist. Interesting, isn't it?

So can we let all that go? Can we forget fair? It only causes war if we don't agree. Can we treat each other with as much politeness and respect as we can muster – or move away? Can we forget about being right, and having rights, and focus on that respect?

It's not not fair! That's right! Isn't that fantastic? So I can define Success however I want to. It will be my challenge to negotiate possibilities with anyone else my goals impact, and that will be a learned skill. Yes!

First read the instructions

A t one stage we had great changes going on in our family life. Wow - only one stage, you say? This one meant a choice of career opportunities, indecision regarding living quarters, schooling and a heap of other ramifications that would result from any one of the above decisions.

One day I arrived at my regular weekly business breakfast, feeling directionless, stressed, out-of-sorts with the whole scene. I needed some clarity – big time! Thankfully, one of my buddies greeted me warmly. "How are you going?" he asked with genuine interest. "OK", I mumbled. "Got a lot going on right now, not sure what's going to happen." There were probably one or two other fairly desolate, self-pitying expressions too embarrassing to recall. He gave me a big smile and an encouraging hug and said, "Yeah, life's a buzz, isn't it? Sometimes you just wish they gave you a list of instructions!"

I gave him a huge hug right back. Because I remembered that we do have a book of instructions. In fact we've got thousands of them. It's all there for us, in all the wonderful words ever written by other strugglers who have found a few simple secrets that worked for them, by gurus and greats who cared enough to help those who would come along after them. In a way, that's one of the reasons I'm writing this – hoping it will help you a little.

I've heard it said before that the ignorant man is not he who cannot read, but rather he who can but doesn't. It absolutely fascinates me that there on my bookshelves, amongst all the former woodpulp and inks, are several hundred lifetimes at least of accumulated wisdom and experience, all recorded and published for my guidance. And now within my very lightweight laptop, I can access almost all the knowledge on the planet!

How could I ignore that? So far I've found an extraordinary amount of help from the instructions I have made the time to look for. I know they'll be there, anytime I go looking again.

'.....the ignorant man is not he wo cannot read, but rather he who can but doesn't.'

It's not just books or search engines, either, that provide the "instructions" we need from time to time.

There is so much we can learn from each other, with the sort of humility you can only possess if you also have real self-love, to have a look for the knowledge that the fellow in front of you comes up with if you give him the chance.

It's always been one of the things about my business and personal world that has amazed me; that week after week I have the opportunity to learn not only from the speakers I get to hear at the various events held in my area, but also from the podcasts, webinars, blogs and newsletters that come through my inbox. At no other time in history has so much guidance and support been available to us.

And that's without considering the simple street-smart wisdom of the people around me. The world is a classroom full of teachers, if I will just open my mind and listen to them. Family, friends, colleagues, leaders and mentors – how could I ever feel lost?

Unless I let my pride get in the way of letting them know that I would like some guidance. And unless I am so unclear of my own goals, my values and my boundaries that I don't know what questions to ask, whose guidance to follow, and what I want the outcome to be - lacking a clear authentic compass of my own. Surely I wouldn't be in that place? Me?

OK, I will share with you, I have been there. Why, you ask, with all that input available? Because I'm human, like all of us. Because the earth moves beneath me, and I try to make it stop. Because although I want peace and comfort, life is shaking me up and I can't find the next step, let alone the goal. Can you relate?

There was a really, really bad time when I could not see out of the Pit. My world was dark and desperate, and my only way of coping was to pretend all was or would be all right, any time soon. If I could just get things back to the way they were, everything would be fine. I could not figure out How, but even worse I could not figure out What Where When or even Why. I could not find my goals, at least any workable ones. I did not have a compass.

But I did have my values and my boundaries – what I stand for in life, and what I won't stand for. I had my breath and my brain, such as it was at the time. I had some sense of purpose, except that I kept beating myself up for not reaching it. Have you ever done that? Please don't.

Because even those dark times have a purpose of their own. We need to know that sense of

'...even those dark times have a purpose of their own.'

44

humility, I think, to really be of service and value to the rest of us who are afraid that no-one will understand our darkness.

I reached out to friends and colleagues. The love and unquestioning support was there. I found teachers, supporters, counsellors and coaches, all willing to share their own journeys

So I guess I have been reminded over the last while that we do have plenty of instructions to follow. We just have to look for them, and know they will find us.

Not rules. Well maybe. My favourite Rule is that All Rules Are Made To Be Broken Including This One.

And no shoulds. I've shared with you that I will never should on myself again.

After the time it took me to recover from that distress and now several years of lightness and brightness – not always easy, but always with faith and hope – I've actually created my own Instructions. This is the first time I have shared them with anyone! Let me know what you think?

1. There are only two states of being. One is love, the other is fear. This love is not erotic, romantic or gooey love. It's full, complete acceptance. A universal unconditional love that transcends and persists regardless of circumstance. Everything that is not love is fear. And I get to choose whether I will live out of love or out of fear.

2. Be trustworthy. That includes honesty, integrity, reliability, and discretion. I was once unkindly accused of gossiping, where my intent was to share a story to make the other person present feel better about themselves. Nevertheless it was not my story to share, and I regret that. It also means that I will say what

I mean and mean what I say. No games. Transparency not manipulation.

3. If I'm not happy, make a choice. Either choose another circumstance, or choose to be happy. M.Scott Peck says that love is a doing word. So is happy. Abraham Lincon said (or so I'm told) that most people are about as happy as they make up their minds to be. I experienced that lesson in a tourist coach travelling around Rome, about 30 years ago. I've never forgotten it. Occasionally my neural wiring gets distorted by other stuff. I can get very sad or even hopeless. I've found sharing that with someone who loves me, helps enormously to restore my clarity. And I choose happy.

4. Victimhood does not belong in my life. I am not a victim, I am a victor. Stuff will always happen. It's my life and I can choose how to deal with it. I want to deal with it with love. Sometimes I forget. Mostly I remember. And I march forward (gently) with my banner flying that says 'Love everything. Welcome it all. We are connected.' Metaphorically of course – all though the banner could be a great idea!

5. Money is the ultimate healer. If there is ever a shortage of money in my life (which has occurred more than once!) I know it's my 'stinking thinking', as the wonderful Zig Ziglar used to say. I need a 'check up from the neck up', because I have 'hardening of the attitudes'. Those words are challenging – and so accurate! It is always my responsibility if finances have fallen. I can not play victim. (See #4) What did I do or not do to cause or create this? One time not long ago someone owed me a lot of money and declared bankruptcy. I was shocked, angry, etc. etc. The real truth was that I knew it would happen, and refused to face it in advance. I might not have been able to change the circumstances but I could have changed my management strategies earlier and avoided some of the pain.

Money management is essential – we need to eat – and it's part of learning to love ourselves.

6.   Right Timing. There is never one right answer. I've learned to 'go inside' and explore my feelings, my motives and intent. You may find that odd. Perhaps it is. I have procrastinated about a lot of things over the years – including rewriting and releasing this book. Yet right now is exactly the right time. So perhaps the 'Procrastination Paradox' as I call it, is simply my coming to terms with a few things. Occasionally I might procrastinate because I'm afraid of doing something and getting a negative outcome. Is that so 'wrong'? Or is it smart? Can I just trust that when it is the 'right' time to do something I will simply do it. And it will work out perfectly.

OK. I've cheated a little. The last one is not really an instruction. It's still in question. My current instruction is to sit with it.

Only this morning I was asked again what I think 'success' is. My answer is that it is achieving something I set out to achieve. Like finishing this book. Or like cooking a delicious omelette. He asked because I think he wonders if his life has been a success. There's no question in my mind, because he has two daughters he is proud of, and four great growing grandsons. Does he still have heaps of money? I don't think so, and I think that's irrelevant. He has enough. But. If he doesn't feel like he has achieved what he wanted to achieve, then he can not claim to be a success. So today, I believe it's very personal, individual and truthful. Only I can say if I am a success.

Yes. Today I have followed my own instructions and met my own measurements. Today I am a success.

Roadblocks and Detours

M uch of my corporate life before I founded my business growth consultancy, was spent in the financial services industry. I was involved in the marketing, training and business development aspects of the investment advisory industry, and I shared my life with one of this country's best investment fund managers. So what? you ask.

I have spent a great deal of time over many years looking at money matters: past, present and to come. And they are matters of great relevance to us all.

What is our economic future? How safe will we be from another crash, or crisis, whether general or personal? What industries or organisations should we look for employment in? What business strategies will support the most success?

I have some shocking news for you.

It is entirely up to you.

Others may well suffer a recession or depression, but whether you do or not is entirely your choice. In every major market correction, there have been sectors that were untouched. Many businesses prospered.

Many people suffered, struggled, then recovered and went on to be more successful than they were before.

You may have heard or read the story of a famous hot dog vendor in the US, who became a business success with his roadside stand. At some distance from his stand and at regular intervals along the highway, he had paid for road signs and posters promising the best and freshest hot dogs available to travellers right there in their cars. His product was good, he met a need, and he promoted his offering very well. People read the signs, stopped ordered and ate, and he prospered – well enough to send his son to an expensive university.

In due course the son returned home, and challenged his father about his extravagant marketing. "Don't you know, Dad, times are tough right now – you're spending way too much on these signs!!" The vendor shook his head, but figured his son must know better. So he withdrew all his signage. Sure enough, according to his son's prediction, his thriving little business failed.

Times may well be tough economically over the next few years. Collectively as nations and individually within our family structures, we have been ignoring many of the basic rules of household management. We have outspent our income, we have borrowed more than we could afford to repay and we have not been setting aside a store for a rainy day. The results of that sort of behaviour in a family sense, and in any nation's economy, are no different.

The important thing to know and to remember when the going gets toughest, is that ultimately, whether you succeed or fail depends entirely on you.

'....ultimately whether you succeed or fail depends entirely on you.'

Many of our planet's business success stories have been written by those who have encountered seemingly impossible obstacles and who, in the fight to overcome them, have developed abilities and strategies that have gone on to take them to the top. Many believe that it is when times are toughest - when everybody else runs for cover - that the opportunities to thrive and grow are most widespread.

I've learned from experience that the most important ingredient is the strength within. You need that knowledge of your own inner resources, and a real conviction that your product or service is of value to others. If you're not sure, get out there and ask your customers. You need humility to listen to feedback and to keep improving. And above all you need a willingness to serve.

'....the most important ingredient is the strength within. '

If you're unable to find anyone to pay you for your skills in your current environment, be willing to change it. Do your research and develop the response-to-need your market is looking for. It sounds simple – it's not, and it's not always easy either. But it's a lot easier than being miserable. Take action, any action, because a body in motion creates energy and that's what you need to keep moving.

You've probably heard it many times, it's not what happens to you in this world, it's your reaction to it that shapes your destiny. It is as true of good times as it is of hard times. W Clement Stone is famous for saying, "there is one thing over which man has absolute, inherent control, and that is his mental attitude". You may not be able to select or control or direct the economic events of your environment, but you can certainly select, control and direct your response to them. And I know you can do it brilliantly.

Isn't it great to know you're in the driver's seat?

The more things change.....

A lot of people I know have been making major changes in their lives. I don't know if it's the weather, the time of life I suppose a lot of us are at right now, or whether it's some mysterious message from the universe telling us all to get up and move three seats to the right and sit down again. I have made a few moves myself in recent months, and thinking back over the year and planning for the next one, my mind was well occupied contemplating change.

We know, don't we, that nothing in existence is permanent. Everything you can think of will change in time. Some things change very quickly - by the second. You, for instance. Others take time - mountains, for example. But nothing exists that will last forever in the same form or substance as you know it now. It will all change.

Yet somehow that is one of the facets of our human existence with which we find it hardest to live. For some reason we cling determinedly to situations, to possessions, and to people, trying to make everything stay just as it is. Even when we know those situations are painful and unpleasant, we tend to experience a reluctance to alter.

What is the result when we try to resist change? Whether it is in our business, our economic climate, our personal lives? Such everyday things as an altered travel arrangement, or a child growing up? We hurt, that's what!

We don't instantly become extinct, like dinosaurs. Although we could, if we resisted long enough!

But we hurt. We suffer anger, frustration, impatience. Our pride is assaulted, we fight back and we can take it to extremes by sending out messages of fury, even hatred. And as most of us know by now that we tend to get our serves returned to us, that only ends up causing more trouble and the cycle continues.

One of the greatest lessons I learned from my amazing teacher Spike is that all of the pain and misery of life comes from hanging on to something that ought to be allowed to pass. Whether it is wanting something too much that you can't have, or not wanting something that you must have, all of the trauma results from simply not allowing things to be as they are.

Easier said than done, you say? I agree.

It starts with self-awareness, and being able to notice when you are trying to resist change. The second a negative feeling comes up, being able to notice it and release it.

We've learned much about the power of meditation. At its simplest, it is an activity that exercises our mind. We practice being still, observing our breath, or focusing on a sound or an image. It's that focus that creates the strength we need. When we begin, it's hard to retain the focus; just like learning to do anything, we improve with practice – and it doesn't take long. Even 5 minutes a day is good. I started with 2!

As distractions enter our mind, we can either observe them gently and return to our focus, or we can use a quick 'cut' instruction to take us back. There is no 'good' or 'bad' meditation – it is all good practice.

Over time, this helps us to stop being reactive with our thought patterns. We get better at noticing our thoughts – that in fact they are not US, they are just our thoughts, and we can choose to change them. That's power!

I've also found that clear goals, values and boundaries really are a huge help. When your direction and purpose is known, you are able to focus on what you are doing and why, and you realise what you can let go of or allow to just turn up.

'....we get better at noticing our thoughts – that in fact they are not US..... and we can choose to change them. '

'....clear formulation of your goals and objectives for every aspect of your life will be your biggest aid. '

Actually, the easiest way to allow, is to just do it easy.

I used to talk a lot about the widely held concept of "no pain, no gain". It was something I had heard at various motivational gatherings and I thought it was pretty logical. Perhaps it just fitted in too with my upbringing where I was taught, like you I'm sure, that you don't get anywhere without really working hard. Football coaches use it a lot, so do some religious bodies, and I know it is used with the utmost sincerity.

What I have now discovered is that although that is absolutely true – hard work is necessary to achieve your goals and objectives - it doesn't' have to be painful! It can be fun! Not flippant, careless, light-hearted, foolish fun, but pleasurable, satisfying, rewarding, stimulating, enjoyable and positive fun.

The pain will come anyway, just because that's the way it is. How we handle it, our attitude to the discomfort of change, will determine our level of achievement. If we can just allow the pain, experience it without judging it, owning it or trying to avoid it, it will pass in its own time.

So any pain is just a possible outcome of change. Change is necessary for you to grow. Growth is the only way you can achieve and succeed.

If you can see change – with any accompanying hurt - as great evidence that you are taking the next step forward, you're doing it easy. Take if from here.

Whatever it is, relate it to the impermanence of all existence and let it go by. The more things change......the more you get to win!

3

RUN YOUR OWN LIFE

Do you know that you can never make a wrong decision? Isn't that a blast? So you need never be afraid to take one again. Or to get rid of hesitation and indecision and non-action - they cause most of our problems for us anyway! Let's start your own personal fan club. Let's say whatever you ever do will be OK, because it will always be your best at that time. And shush-up that little voice of past experience, or OPO (other people's opinions) saying you can't. You can if you want to! Absolutely! It's your script, you know.

Don't sweat the small stuff

Sometimes you find the most amazing things in the most unlikely places, don't you? I have developed over the years an illogical compulsion to always read my horoscope wherever I see it written up. I say illogical because with the greatest respect to those who seriously study our planetary movements and their effects on our life paths, it does not seem likely to me that one twelfth of the world's population will experience the same thing at the same time. Maybe they will. Who am I to be a sceptic? But for some reason these columns nearly always reflect pretty accurately what I am going through at the time. Amazing. So I read them.

One day I found something I particularly liked. This one thing has made all the years of illogical behaviour worthwhile.

"At all times, and in all situations, you must remember that fearing the unknown is a waste of time. Life now offers exactly what you need. No event is more than you can handle, and all that is required is acceptance".

Like it? It's a life saver!!

A few years ago I had a big decision to make – whether to run as a candidate for President of my professional association. A good friend gave me a priceless piece of his wisdom, which has given me courage and encouragement on many occasions since. He said, "Catherine, you can never make a wrong decision." Wow! Was that a relief! That one line removed more fear and worry from my life than you can imagine.

You may argue, of course. There are some gross errors made by deluded and criminal minds that most certainly do not seem like right decisions to any of us. That wasn't the point.

His point was that for most of us, indecision and non-action are the greatest cause of our problems, rather than the actual decisions and actions taken. The logic is that everything we do, every place we get to, we learn something more and grow in the doing and the getting to. Our normal common human fears of change, of failure and of success, which paralyse us with worry into wrinkled little old statues, are the real obstacles to our growth and development; not the possible outcomes of the steps we fear to take.

'....indecision and non-action are the greatest cause of our problems.'

There's a lot of concern in my world about stress. It's real, very real! I see it in my friends and sometimes my family, and I feel it too. I've designed stress management programs, and of course as a behavioural scientist I've researched intensely on the topic.

Did you know that stress is a major contributing factor in 75% of human illness? That's a lot, huh? Are you aware that over $200 billion annually is lost in the US alone through poor productivity due to stress? Does it concern you that the ten most common terminal illnesses can be traced to lifestyle and stress? It has even now been found to be a significant factor in unhealthy weight gain.

NOW are you worried - and if not, why not!

You're not, are you? Good.

One of my favourite Abraham Lincoln quotes is that people are just about as happy as they make up their mind to be. I think it's the same with stress. We are just about as stressed as we make up our minds to be.

Before you scream at me (in your stress response) and get violently angry because I am suggesting you can control your own stress, please take three deep breaths and chill. Then you can call me anything you choose. Except you won't want to.

So, you know I'm a behavioural scientist. That means that I work hard to understand how and why people respond to stimuli, so that ideally they can become more aware of their own triggers and manage them. Consciously at first, and eventually automatically. Making for easier lives and better outcomes.

So can you take a minute to think about what (or who) triggers your stress response? It's always because the world is not the way you want it to be – either in the moment or over the long term.

You have a couple of choices in that scenario. One is to keep resisting the way things are, fairly ineffectually it seems, and stay stressed. How is that working for you so far? All good? Happy? Loving life? Really?

The other is to remember that no-one can stress you. It's YOUR stress response. You get to choose whether you relax and chant (or shout) your mantra – which can often take the form of 'Get $&*#!!%%(!' – or one of my favourite statements "I am always all I ever need to be". Or whether you freak out and run round in circles complaining that life's not fair. Both are fine! It's just a matter of what you believe is the best response, for you and for the challenge at hand.

For a long time I thought that stressing meant I cared.

I would be worried if I got to Thursday and hadn't panicked yet about whether I would get everything done that week. Sometimes I would worry that I wasn't worrying. (I do know people who pretend to be worried because they are worried other people will think they ought to be worried about something}. A full desk with an impossible schedule meant I was important, needed and at the same time completely useless. Does that make sense to you? Of course it doesn't! But it might be familiar.

It makes sense to me that each of us is in charge of what we agree to. Sometimes we agree to something that later turns out to be impossible. When we are authentically living our truth, in fearlessness, we are able to be honest about that, and negotiate the best way ahead with anyone else involved. That includes our employers, perhaps our employees. Our kids and probably our life partners. And anyone else we are trying to keep happy. It's absolutely not our job to make them happy – it's our job to be honest, to do our best with integrity, and to throw away our need to please when it comes from a place of fear. Which it usually does.

Our work is to love ourselves enough to speak our truth. To allow others to speak theirs. We can accept that or reject it. But we can't deny it. We can learn more by listening too. Sometimes that helps to remove stressful responses. I've learned that I can keep learning, expand my perspectives and discover a higher way of thinking that doesn't leave room for me to be stressing. Or sweating or even mild perspiration.

The first step is to decide that you don't intend to sweat the small stuff. As they say – it's all small stuff.

The second step is to actually do something. Or not do something.

A teaser I love to ask clients goes "Four frogs were sitting on a log and one of them decided to jump off. How many were left?" The answer of course is four. The restless one decided to jump off – he didn't necessarily do it. Come on! How often have you decided to do something – and not done it? The answer for me is 'heaps'.

So the doing is essential, or nothing will change.

The best thing to do? Breathe. Typically when we are stressed, we breathe less. Our lungs get less oxygen, our brain is denied its essential nutrient, we get tired and foggy – and we've already considered the vile effect that has on our wellbeing. So breathe. Deeply, frequently. Loving it. Hang on – do you have time for breathing? Oh, of course you do. Or you'll die. Fast or slow, if you don't breathe you will die. Sorry, but that's a fact.

Breathe. Slowly and deeply. Quietly for one minute. Then you can relax.

We act more reasonably, more happily and successfully when we are relaxed. We make faster, smoother decisions, which will inevitably lead us in an appropriate direction, because we can allow our unlimited mind to use some of its potential. We can actually develop real turbo power in our lives - all by relaxing and using less effort.

Feeling tense? Stressed? Have a look where it's coming from. Is it past events or possible future events that are going through your head? They

'.....We act more reasonably, more happily and successfully when we are relaxed. '

are both unreal, drop them. The only reality is right now. And right now is all yours, with complete control to handle, as you will.

As the late great Dr Wayne Dyer told us; it makes no sense to worry about things you can control. And it makes no sense to worry about the things you can't control. Yes?

Energy, pure and transformed energy, is what this world is made of. It's what your life is made of too. There's so much more of it, so very much more, when you quit worrying. Just give it up for today. Then for tomorrow. Then the next day.

And each day will be a success.

Do you really want to change the world?

Isn't it interesting how easy it is to say yes to that question? Hasn't it been a time for provoking that?

Even if you don't burn with a feverish mission to reform this or that, even if you don't have a cause you pursue with passion, it's just so tempting to wish you could change something we don't like, isn't it?

Yet, given the chance, we baulk at it, don't we?

Because to change the world, we first have to change us! Oh no! Anything but that! I'm fine just the way I am, thanks - don't change me. Besides, that's uncomfortable, and I'd rather avoid discomfort at all costs.

As if – you're perfect, it's everyone and everything else that's screwed up. Right?

Sometimes we're just deluded, don't you agree?

If you are at all dissatisfied with where you are now, you know the story. We really need to get real and get this. The reality is that unless we are prepared to change something about our life - work habits, disciplines, personal fitness, whatever it is we're dissatisfied with - we are stuck. Stuck firm. And we will just go on getting whatever we're getting now. As we know, one well-known definition of insanity attributed to Albert Einstein is when we keep on doing what we have always done and expect a different outcome.

Maybe you are stuck in 'metaphorical mud' – where we know we are stuck, it's not comfortable and we're not seeing the world the way we want it to be. Even if you know that you can get out of stuck, it will be an effort. Mud can be hard work.

Maybe you are stuck in some loose sand – it's way easier to walk through than deep thick mud, but it still needs your commitment.

'....unless we are prepared to change something about our lives – we are stuck.'

Or I've talked with some people who actually think they are stuck in concrete. Seriously. They are in pain, they are voluntarily suffering, they complain a lot, they don't want any solutions or suggestions because they want to be right, and there's often a pay-off for them in being in pain. They are often rewarded with attention, with sympathy, with praise even. And they are going to stay stuck in concrete because it feels better to them than the risks they would experience in getting out of it.

I'm not suggesting you're stuck at all. You may be completely footloose and free, ready to act immediately on anything at all you see that isn't giving you the results you want. But in my experience (and that's been extensive) we nearly all are stuck somewhere.

We usually have a fairly clear self-definition. Most of us can complete the sentence "I am someone who…….." fairly easily. And some take it to extremes and become rigid. I remember travelling with a friend who kept saying "I'm not a chicken person…" when it was suggested for dinner. Or "No, I'm not a red wine person…" which I found funny. It was a good mirror for me to see where I might be stuck in a long-term habit, in my points of view, or in bias whether conscious or unconscious.

I've shared this already in other chapters, because I really think it's useful. It's the quote that has inspired me most around this issue always has been from Jim Rohn. "If you don't like it, move!! You're not a tree!"

'….become more flexible, more willing to be who I need to be, to live in that better world.'

I've learned that to have my world the way I want it to be, daily and for the long term, I have needed to become more flexible, more willing to be who I need to be to live in that better world. I need some new and different thinking and feeling, some effort, so I can shake off the sand, throw off the mud, or even cut through the concrete.

Like me, I bet you know people who don't take responsibility for creating their 'better world'. Is it you? Do you ever say "Maybe someday things will get better"? Yes, they will. When you get better. It's an oldie but a goodie – if you do what you've always done, you'll get what you've always got. It really needs change to make a difference in your life.

One of the things we sometimes have to deal with is our really weird innate defensiveness when change is suggested, either by others or by ourselves. It seems that we feel we have to stand up for whatever we have been doing in the past, even fiercely justify it, as a defence against correction. As if that correction implies that what we have been doing is bad, or just not good enough. It's as if we feel changing something is proof that we were failing previously. Sound familiar?

When we look at it logically, we know full well that what we were doing previously was fine - for then! But now is now, and now needs a different approach to then. Now I have a specific goal or a different commitment, or even an insight - and then I didn't, or it wasn't important enough.

Whenever we approach change, the talkative little devil inside us goes into overdrive. Somehow that voice does its best to convince us - we can't, we never did before, we never do, we're not….. If you hear it, give it its moment, and add consciously - "until now!"

"I get up every morning and go for a half hour walk in the park." ("You do not, you never did, you can't get up in the morning…") "Until now." Little Devil only knows the past, it doesn't know the present or the future, so it can't comment if you bring NOW into it. Give it a go, and see if I'm right. LD loves the past, it can justify anything. But we're no longer living in it. So any conditions good or bad that come up from that 'story' have actually gone. We can either recreate them in every moment, or we can choose different.

Another useful understanding to grasp is the realisation that maybe there are no good and bad views about what went before. It's just a matter of shifting your position to get a better view. Nothing's wrong with the former position, it's just that this one could offer a better alternative. The car you bought two years ago was exactly the right car for you to buy at that time, yes? You're trading it in now, because now is a different time with a different need. You've evolved. Nothing wrong with the last car back then. You just want to drive a different vehicle now. Like your life!

It takes a bit of guts. And understanding our built-in resistance to change.

While our clever logical neo-cortex wants to change, our emotively driven limbic brain system is not quite so sure. And our reptilian brain, responsible for homeostasis, our survival, so wants everything to stay the same to ensure stability – it's freaking out, and will do everything it can to prevent our change acceptance.

Yet we really need to gather a preparedness to accept and embrace the necessary change for your better world, and make it part of your character. With continual learning, curiosity, celebration for every step taken. You don't necessarily have to live in a constant state of flux, but rather with an openness and flexibility to keep exploring. Sometimes it IS fun to change just for change's sake. It does relieve tension and boredom and presents a fresh outlook for current achievement. Try moving your office or home furniture around; just to see the new views that present themselves.

And one of the major benefits is the passing of attachments. ALL of the gripes you and I ever have, are based on our desire to have things the way we want them, and not be willing to just allow things (and people) to be the way they are. When we know we can really let go of our need to control and grasp, when we are relaxed about change in our own and other's lives and circumstances, it's a breeze. I see this so much in relationships – which have been a major learning platform for me! "He should….."!! Why can't she……??" etc. etc. I don't believe in shoulds, they are usually unsupportable, and always someone else's agenda. He is being who he is, and it's your choice to negotiate arrangements, or to stop being a tree. She will do what she does in her own truth. Don't you want that for her? You can then act from your truth, being and doing what is right for you.

There is nothing wrong with you. There never was. You are amazing, magnificent. You have always done your best, with what you had, however you could. And no-one has the right to say otherwise. You made your choices, and they have brought you to where you are. Now you might want to make different choices, to get to a new place – but only if you want to. And if you do.....

Just for today, try on some small changes. Do something different. Sleep on the other side of the bed. Put the other leg into your trousers first. Leave milk out of your coffee - or put it in. Whatever. Of course it will be yuk. It's unfamiliar! All change is. Give it a go, just for fun! And the new you will know you can do anything, whatever it is.

You are a success walking. That's how we change the world.

When you're over it

I can't believe the number of people I've spoken to lately who are telling me that they're exhausted. In this world where we don't walk many places, where our food is cooked in a few minutes and we only have to turn a handle to get hot water! How on earth did our forebears survive!!

Let's blame the pace of life, shall we? Anything but ourselves, huh?

It's easy for me to get re-energised and inspired by a seminar or webinar on goal-setting, or branding, or strategy review. Somehow the thought of a different path can get my energy up. At least for a while. The new goals get written up and mapped out into action plans and it doesn't take long to get started. Full of zest and enthusiasm, belief in myself and commitment to producing personal and business growth for my clients, I get really wound up and take off. So do you, I know, whatever your work or service is.

Then what happens? A few weeks later, how is it that we get that drop in energy?

From every perception I can put together, it's almost inevitable.

Because within nearly every one of us, there is a fabulously efficient recording device switched on in our minds, happily playing back to us all our previous recordings. Tracks that say "I'm tired, I should have, I didn't, I ought to, I can't, he thinks, she said, I'm too busy, I failed at that last time, I'm not good at this, I never win, they'll never buy from me..." and so on.

So how can we, poor darlings, fight all that? It's impossible! Aren't we just wonderful even keeping going? No wonder we develop all that guilt and inadequacy and self-doubt. No wonder almost as soon as we start work we feel worn out.

So let's take it nice and easy now, and see if we can work out some strategies for making life a little easier on ourselves. Are you ready?

Here are my recommendations:

> **'.....undermining our every intent is an unseen belief that it's not possible. '**

Firstly let's start by checking those goals, targets and objectives. Are they real? Not just in terms of being physically achievable within a specific, realistic time frame. But more especially in terms of our existing beliefs, values and opinions about ourselves. Are they aligned? For a lot of us this is a major problem: that incredibly effective digital mind-recorder is efficiently and often silently counteracting all the conscious commitment and affirmation we so determinedly make. We 'think' that we want something, and we do our best to go about making it happen. But undermining our every intent is an unseen belief that it's not possible.

Sabotaging us at every turn, a digital recording of our parent, our teacher, our 'friends' even, reminding us who we are (which is not true) and what we can't do. Why? Because it's part of our survival mechanism to avoid danger and reconvene the tribe, where no-one stands out and everyone keeps their head down. You know how important that was, in historical circumstances, some of them quite recent.

There are a couple of ways to fix that, of course.

One way is to alter the goals and targets so they do fit. That's the easiest, and I think it's our customary fallback pattern. We actually abandon or downgrade our goals and dreams, so they don't challenge our recorded beliefs. Sometimes at the behest of our friends and family, who want us to stay just the same because they love us that way. Or they love how we make them feel right now, but if we improved our circumstances we might not have the same impact. We could even be challenging to them. So minimising our life vision can be an almost daily occurrence. You too?

This might not be what you want - although it may be. At least if you're aware of it, and you choose to preserve the status quo so no-one gets uncomfortable with us, it's your choice.

The other way is to alter or eliminate those beliefs, or values, or opinions. You need to be very firmly committed to that, it it's what you want. There are some great techniques I can recommend and some great teachers of them. Surface methods are often not enough.

One of the best tools in my experience is The Sedona Method. I'm not a facilitator, I don't receive any benefit for this, I just find it works.

I've qualified as an NLP Master Practitioner with three schools. Why? They keep finding new data and methodologies, and I love to keep learning. So I know how well NLP can help in this area. Just make sure you have a reputable practitioner, with a very good track record.

I'm also a big fan of The Breakthrough Experience as taught by Dr John Demartini. Phenomenal logical technology that rewires our neural pathways and gives us a completely positive understanding. It's not 'woo woo'. It's practical and powerful.

If anyone tells you that changing beliefs is difficult, be careful what you listen to and what you agree with. Because THAT's a belief in itself, and beliefs are always self-fulfilling prophecies. They have to be, or we would not be able to function.

Secondly, it is fairly easy to demonstrate a fall in physical energy when negative thoughts are held in your mind, when you are around negative miserable people, or when you accept and live a lie. I do it on stages and platforms by using kinesiology. It's not a circus trick (which I was once accused of), it's a thoroughly researched experience. So if you really want to stop feeling exhausted and live with the highest energy possible, you have two choices again.

Brew some coffee and drink several cups a day. Double your Vitamin B intake. Swallow some sugar. These and many other energy-boosting techniques were part of my life some years back, when I was raising my son alone, running a couple of professional associations, doing my Master's degree and growing my consulting training and speaking businesses.

How did that work out? Non-Hodgkins Lymphoma diagnosis in 2001 with 18 months to live as the oncologist's forecast. Clearly I'm still here – but it was a big scare. I had to learn the impact of not loving myself, of pushing this precious body beyond its capacity to perform, and relying on external stimuli to get through the stress and struggles of every day.

These days I think there are much better answers.

One is to work on those belief systems. You are 100% responsible for your response (of course) to every thing that will happen in your life. You can respond to an event with an old belief pattern and therefore an old behaviour. Or you can rewire your responses in a number of ways – including all those I've just shared with you, and a lot more.

A second answer is to completely avoid any negative people and conversations. I had to learn how to do that. Because some of them are people in my family whom I love! I know now how to leave a conversation that doesn't suit me. There is no point in arguing, or trying to defeat negativity with logic if the person is not open to it. I've found that saying "You may be right – but my point of view is……." and then leaving. Not hanging around to have more negativity fiercely thrusted at me! Life's too short – and it will get even shorter if you hang out with misery.

My home and office are in an absolutely glorious part of this country. I look out over the Coral Sea, my regional city is big enough to have all the facilities I could ever want, the weather is magnificent for me all year round, there is comparatively little traffic and both the air and water are clean. Yet every day I hear someone local complaining about something. The tourists don't, they see what a Paradise it is. But those of us who live here? There's always something for them to moan or whine about. It's a continual challenge for me. Here's the solution I developed (don't laugh!)

Tucked away in my imagination is a full body condom. I mentally position it over the crown of my head and let it drop down enclosing my whole body with a comfortable fit. It's totally transparent, so no-one can see it, although I know it has a kind of rainbow shimmer to it. And I am fully protected against anything anyone can throw at me. I can smile, be gracious, be relaxed and generous even. I'm not affected by negative energy, physically mentally or emotionally.

Occasionally I'll forget to use it. I can (but I won't) share some fairly recent painful experiences which left me reeling. So it does rely on my presence of mind to pull it out of my imagination and create the protection. Is this weird? Do you think we should have put a warning on the book cover?

Whenever you have dissonance or disappointment in your life, where behaviour doesn't match up to expectations (whether it's your own or anyone else's) you have two choices again.

Change the behaviour. Or change your expectations. Either could be valid. What isn't valid is the guilt, the resentment, the distress, the anger from not doing either one or the other.

You know, you really are terrific. You never did do anything that wasn't right at the time, given all the circumstances, the influences on you and the learning curve you were going through. And you never will. You're growing and stretching and everything you are is your choice.

But get real. Stop pretending you want to be what you are not. Your life actually does reflect what you have chosen. Love yourself, love your choices, love your outcomes – and then choose and act differently if you really want to. Knowing that truly, a lot of the people who want you to want more are just trying to sell you a new course or some more coaching. (Ouch, did I really just write that?)

> ‘Your life actually does reflect what you have chosen....’

Maybe you are enough. Maybe you have enough. Maybe you do enough. And maybe – just maybe – today will also present you with new challenges to learn from and new success to enjoy.

Rock around the clock!

No, this is not about Bill Haley and the Comets and their 1950's hit, and it's not about rock'n'roll dancing. Then again, maybe it is.

I've been thinking about time. How it works, how we use it, in fact, even what it is. Because it's always been a truisim for me that we learn most when we teach, and I figure a lot of things out as I write about them, I've decided to inflict of few of my ideas and reflections on you. Thank you so much for reading this!

I have to tell you that many of my friends and family will howl with hysterics when they see me writing about time. Because despite the best efforts of many expert guides and teachers in my life, it's always been a challenge for me to fit in everything I want to do.

Maybe that's the case for you too. Maybe you, too are a committed, dedicated, goal-directed, hard-working, self-disciplined person for whom the world holds so many joys and exciting opportunities that cramming them all in causes that old clock to rock nonstop! So thank you for allowing me to share some viewpoints I find valuable.

Of course, if you're one of those wonderful people who is always on time, always organised to the minute and never has to worry about being late, just skip this bit. (And stop judging the rest of us.)

Firstly, I have discovered that just as our physicists are telling us, time is a total illusion. It actually doesn't exist, except in our minds.

Doubt me? How often have you been immersed in your favourite activity for what turns out to be hours, when you knew for a fact it was only minutes? And how many "hours" have you sat in doctors' waiting rooms, even though each hour turned out to be just ten minutes?

So perhaps we should just accept at the outset that time is a concept, with a man-made measurement tool called the clock, that manifests as very flexible for some of us. And if we waste any of it getting upset about that, it's a self-defeating act. (If any of this sounds totally unscientific, of course it is – other than as a phenomenological heuristic narrative. Get over it, it's just a perspective.)

Secondly, that our flexible perspective of time is directly related to our own internal value-driven priorities. Not the priorities others have given us, but those we inwardly - and sometimes even secretly or unconsciously - hold firmly for ourselves. Those priorities that really are what we value most in life. Our values.

Your employer can send you to as many time management courses as you can find the time for, but until you've personally chosen to do the things you are told you 'should' schedule to do, nothing will work. Until we see something as important to us, we will not give it our time.

You will always be late for appointments if there is a secret fear of failure, or success, attached to them. You will always be running late with deadlines you don't really want to keep. You will never find the time to work on all those boring papers and reports you have piled up on your desk, to empty your inbox or to read all the magazines you have in your reading pile or file. And you simply can never do all the things you have agreed to do, to please everyone else. Why? You don't really want to.

And desire will triumph over discipline every time.

'.....desire will triumph over discipline every time. '

The answer? Just as with other desired outcomes, if you are not getting what you want, either change your expected outcome or change your attitude to it. Create the desire, if you can. Changing the behaviour will only be temporary if you don't.

I've always found especially useful the guidance from M. Scott Peck that Love is a Doing Word. (I love it so much you may find it elsewhere in this book!) So you can choose to Do the things that show you Love someone, if you want to. Or you can choose to Do the things you already Love. (Just be aware you may not get paid for them.) Or – you can actually choose to Love what you perceive you need to do, to meet the other important values in your life, like looking after your children, putting a roof over your heads, and downright paying for joyful experiences if that's a goal.

I have, in fact, run time management training. Not often! But I've worked out what works, and I'm happy to share it. And it all comes down to the key to most success patterns; Work out what you Want. You can be given all the tools and techniques in the world, but if you don't know what you want, you'll do a lot of rocking around without ever getting to it.

Determine your own priorities. Living by those imposed by others will only cause you confusion, make you feel pressured and imprisoned, and lead you to guilt and resentment. That's why I don't believe in 'shoulds'. Choosing your own time allocations will lead you to fulfilment and satisfaction.

Think about this one – just great for the libertarians among you; maybe if you don't want to do something, it's best if you don't. Bit extreme, you say? I know if sounds like it, but when you decide to live up to your own priorities and deadlines, it makes more sense. And I firmly believe that the word 'should' always demonstrates someone else's agenda, not your own.

Yes, of course we have commitments and responsibilities to others, and they have some claims on our time. We allow that. We choose it. Then it's our deadline, not theirs, isn't it? We can't play victim, and be powerless, and cry that we don't have enough time.

Somehow when we're doing what we want, even though the hours feel like minutes, we manage to fit more into them.

'Somehow when we're doing what we want....we manage to fit more in...'

Have you ever felt really stressed doing what you want to be doing? Bet you haven't. You get stressed doing what others want you to do, when it isn't your choice. Being a victim. So living up to your own priorities can remove stress too.

Over recent years I had the guilts about procrastinating. I've already shared that I nearly killed myself by doing too much. Several years of illness and recovery showed me how to live my best life with ease and grace. So I will share with you also that I let the pendulum swing back to the other side, and for quite a while, did very little. Then, when I was well again, I brought the old whip out once more (metaphorically speaking, of course!). Suddenly my desk was piled with 'stuff' again. I had at least five projects on the go, and began to realise that I was playing old games and making commitments to others and to myself that in my saner moments I knew I couldn't keep. No, I could have kept them if I worked at my old killer pace, 24/7. But the very serious vow I made to take good care of myself, reminded me not to do that. Good, you say. Yes – and the commitments were still there.

One of my values is to keep promises. I will always keep the promises I make to others. And if I can't, I negotiate a revised deadline. It was the commitments I made to myself that were bothering me. There was a full-on battle between my goal deadlines and my need to rest. My self-care promise won. But instead of negotiating a revised deadline with myself, I just called it procrastination and felt guilty. Duh! Do you see how ridiculous that was? I was simply not following the logical and respectful process I'd put in place for others. Yes, I was delaying doing the things I told myself I would do. But you know what? Nobody died. It was not a life-threatening situation. It took me longer than I'd planned, to finish this book, to create my online courses, to script and create the videos I wanted to post. And everyone survived, including me. And you.

So now I treat time with the respect it deserves. Which – when it involves other people's time - is very high. And it definitely deserves as much respect when it is my play time, my fitness time, my rest time and my meditation.

And as for dancing… that's how it feels when you're on the move doing things you love doing, with love for yourself as well. That's success.

You can't afford the luxury
of a negative thought!

---

hen I first heard that quote, (the title of a book by John
Roger) I disagreed violently. Because for me, negative
thinking is not a luxury, it's a poverty.

Then I read the book. On the cover, it says that it's intended for people
with life-threatening illness - including life itself. That was a shock!

But just for the moment, let's get back to negative thoughts. They're
everywhere, aren't they? Don't you hear them all around you?

It's the government, you see. It's the economy. It's the property market.
Somehow it's always either too fast or too slow. It's the commoditiy
prices. It's the cost of living. It's all bad news. It's on TV, it's online,
in the papers, on the radio. And most recently it's been the conspiracy
theorists.

I'm closely acquainted with a very successful investment expert. Right
now, he's busy. He sniffs a falling market and buys in. He sees something
starting to move up in value and he sells it, leaving something in it for
the next person. He's a counter-cyclical investor.

Catherine Palin-Brinkworth

He knows that when people are frightened, they'll panic. They make rash decisions, believe the worst, and actually fulfil their own expectation. They'll sell out of potentially valuable situations out of sheer fear and overlook the fundamental value and real potential. They are the lemmings - follow the crowd, believe in the bad news, and ultimately make it happen as a self-fulfilling prophecy.

Are you a lemming or a leader? Are you a player or a stayer?

Because in any economic climate, the difference is enormous. Either you can find all the problems, worry or complain about them, use them as a serious excuse for not taking action and become a genuine victim of the circumstances - or you can look realistically and shrewdly at the inhibiting factors around you, find ways to overcome them, keep focusing on the perennial benefits of your product or service, staying and lasting while others fade around you. There is a lot of potential market growth in that.

'...follow the crowd, believe in the bad news, and ultimately make it happen as a self-fulling prophecy.'

A couple of other very successful people impressed me this week.

One was in real estate. He told me he had seen it all, the good times and the bad.

"But somehow," he said, "I'm confident in the turning of the wheel. Challenging climatic conditions have been and gone before and I will be there when they come and go again.

"In the meantime, I'll build and service my client base. People always buy and sell houses, and I'm going to make sure they buy them from me.'

He builds his database, he stays in touch, and he cares.

The other was a master, a wise builder of men and women over some years. He had seen cycles come and go too. He knows what it feels like to have to face the market with our weaknesses, our call reluctance, our yielding tendencies and he knows how easy it is for us to buckle under when the going gets tough. But he also knows the inherent value of his product, and he helps all his people to know and remember that, too, throughout his organisation.

And that value is there in his product, year in and year out, regardless of what is happening in the economy. It's a good product that continually evolves to meet the needs of the market, and when his customers need and want it, they find the money.

There are quite a few people like these two around. They are the business leaders, the stayers, the professionals. The success stories. They don't do it easy. They believe in themselves, and in their product and service. They don't deny reality, but they work with it, finding the good and developing that.

Stay away from the Negative Neds and Nellies - do they really have any constructive good to offer you? Commit yourself to mix with successful achieving people, read good books, sit in on webinars and seminars, and fill your mind with the possibilities and opportunities that exist at all times - especially these times.

Through her work with A Course In Miracles, Marianne Williamson tells us that there are only two states of emotional energy – love and fear. It's been fascinating for me to realise how much time most of us spend in fear. It drives us 'below the line' with distress, anger, blame, shame, despair, and even 'common garden variety' guilt. Above the line is learning, gratitude, and sheer joy.

About 15 years ago I developed a model for our emotional energy expenditure. My research had shown me that a lack of physical energy was often caused by a drain of emotional energy. It's often manifested in clinical depression.

There's a line across the middle of a diamond shape. It's 'The Line'. It is labelled Authority. Because it's where you get to Author your own life by the choices you make. It is unemotional and objective, observing cause and effect. The key phrase is 'That's interesting'.

1. The triangle below The Line is negative emotional energy. It's fear driven. Right at the bottom is a place called The Pit. You'll know it if you've been there. It's dark and you can't find any way out. So you just want to sleep, or cry in pain.

2. The way out, to the next step upwards, is Denial. Usually not accepted or applauded, but very useful, because it can get us out of The Pit and towards The Line.

3. The next step is Blame. Because it is socially acceptable for us to be in a bad place if we have someone to blame. Unfortunately a lot of people stay stuck there, and create a negative feedback loop down to The Pit and back.

4. If we can hang out with the discomfort of self-awareness, we'll move to the next step which is Shame. We know we have gotten ourselves to this place, from earlier choices. We don't like being there! But it is a most healthy and helpful step, as long as we don't stay there but move quickly through it. There's no need for Shame. And when we can release it, we go fast.

5. It leads to the final step below The Line. That step is called Guilt. It's the most commonly stuck-to step on the model. We are in fact often rewarded for Guilt. By those who want to control you, and influence you to believe you 'should' be doing what they have told you to do. It's your choice.

6. The Line is a beautiful place of freedom. You know it's your call to live up to your own standards as you progress towards better outcomes. You, and you alone, are the Author, the Authority, over your own life. The only feedback is what works, and what doesn't, with no judgement, only curiosity.

7. The step above The Line is Learning. Every experience teaches us something – and all that matters is that we are aware, conscious and committed to the best outcomes for ourselves and those we impact.

8. Then of course we are flying up to the step of Gratitude! Because when we know Learning, we're grateful, even when it's been uncomfortable and possibly tragic. There is always something to be thankful for.

9. The step beyond, when we have embraced learning and gratitude, is Joy. It's inevitable. And it's delicious!

10. Then the top of the upper triangle is The Peak. It's actually quite easy to reach when we relinquish Guilt and keep moving upwards in energy. It may or may not be sustainable. I think we move up and down the Emotional Energy model in various segments of our life at various times. But I know that when we move to Authority, we are back in the positive.

Recognising the negative fearful thought is the essential starting point, and that takes

'Recognising the negative fearful thought is the essential starting point, and that takes courage.......'

83

courage. Recognition without self-criticism, with encouragement and assurance. That's self-leadership.

And that's the gift we give ourselves for luxury. A luxury we can all afford.

That of course, is success.

4

FREEDOM & FOCUS

Every privilege we have carries a responsibility.
Every choice creates a decision - and carries a risk.
If you will have freedom, you must take risks.
And you need courage.
Really knowing the desired outcome is a great help!
Take a deep breath, hold the dream and then...just do it.

The free gift that isn't

What a wealth of choice there is around us!

How many times already today have you had to stop and make a decision? Which one, which way, what time, will I or not…it's almost constant, if you think about it. It can definitely be overwhelming at times.

I'm told it has been measured on electro-encephalographs that at the time of making a decision the human brain goes momentarily insane. Right off the chart. We simply can't stand having to choose. After all, what if we're wrong?

That's why trusted suppliers, coaches, mentors and advisers can be so important to us: to truly help us to identify our needs and our goals, and then to help us through that decision-making process into a commitment that's right for us. Whether it's a hairdresser or a business deal, a pair of shoes or a car, a cruise or a career.

Our fear of making a decision can seriously inhibit our lives. The "no" safety twitch takes over, we get scared stiff about the outcome and whether or not we'll regret it later. Better to not make any decision, we think, than to make a wrong one. If any of this sounds familiar to you, keep it in mind when you're next trying to persuade anyone else to do anything. They'll most likely be going through their own mental spasms.

I have often heard people actually grumbling about this right to choose. I've complained occasionally myself. Too many choices. How can I carry all this responsibility? Why do I always have to decide?

The grumblers are right. The freedom to choose does carry the responsibility of the outcome. And yes, it can be draining. Going momentarily insane several times a day can really wear you out!

But consider the alternative.

How would you like to live in a world where you could not choose where to live? Where there was no choice of school systems for your children? Where you couldn't choose your job, your values, your life partner, even your spiritual values? Supermarket shelves with only one brand of everything and the only choice to buy or not to buy? To eat or not to eat?

> '....The freedom to choose does carry the responsibility of the outcome. '

Most of us simply can't imagine living without our daily freedom to choose and that is why we take it so much for granted. We even resent it.

We had an election a little while ago in my part of the world. There were lines of people waiting for part of the day at our voting booth, and although some obviously frail people were taken straight through, many of us had to stand in line for our turn to vote. I was flabbergasted that so many people complained, whined, grizzled and didn't want to wait. Ten minutes was too long for them to allocate from their lives to make their choice for our government.

And yet elsewhere in the world people have died for the very right to do this.

Others in the line spent their time bemoaning the quality of the candidates and decrying the system. So I dared to ask a few (because I'm like that) whether they belong to any political party or were contributing to perhaps improving matters. Because you usually can't change things from the outside. The answer was always no.

I think it's sad. A mentor taught me that "He has the right to criticise who has the heart to help". Otherwise you're just a whiner and a blamer.

The real reflection for me, though, whether we are talking politically or just in terms of our daily life patterns, is that we have the most enormous freedom. If you were able to buy this book and read it, you are part of a very privileged world. We were born with this privilege, most of us have not done anything to earn it, and unless we abuse it for the ill of our neighbours, no one will take it from us.

This freedom has come at a great cost over the centuries. Our forebears have fought many battles – for territory, for survival, for the right to vote. To be able to own property, to get an education and medical care. To choose our own life partners, regardless of race, religion or gender. It has been hard won. And in that, it carries responsibilities.

James Allen wrote in "As a Man Thinketh", a literary essay that has influenced us since 1903, that our freedom of thought provides us with all the tools we need for a rich and happy life.

Mind is the Master power that moulds and makes,
And Man is Mind, and evermore he takes
The tool of Thought, and, shaping what he wills,
Brings forth a thousand joys, a thousand ills: —
He thinks in secret, and it comes to pass:
Environment is but his looking-glass.

Funkadelic, Gucci Mane and Marilyn Manson are just a few songwriters and cultural influencers who have used Allen's words as inspiration. It is all there for us, if we will apply the power we own to our thoughts, and therefore our outcomes.

My poor son got very tired of hearing about choices and consequences when he was growing up, but I still think it was the only way to have him develop wise choices and self-discipline. I remember him at 6 or 7 coming to me for a decision. I discussed with him the range of choices, and what each of them would mean, and the little man stamped his foot and said "Choices!! I'm sick of choices!" I had to agree.

Use it or lose it – we know that's true for our physical muscle. It seems to me that it fits for freedom too.

Yes, it's an incredibly valuable free gift. With two aspects to it.

1. One is that I have the life I choose to live, the people I choose to be around, in a location I find most pleasurable. I am continually grateful. It's not always comfortable, but it always reflects my choices.

'...Use it or lose it.... that fits for freedom, too.'

89

2. So the other aspect is its price. The price of being responsible, of being intelligent and thinking through the choices we are free to make, and the consequences of them. I can't think of anything more important right now, than to be aware of that.

Please think about it. Not just now, but all the time.

And will you please help others – particularly your children and their children - to understand the great gift of the freedom of choice, and the joy of being able to constantly go momentarily insane! Even if they stamp their feet!

We are not victims, unless we choose to be. Even if we can not at present escape our circumstances, we can change our mind about them. History is full of remarkable people who overcame massive obstacles, simply through choosing to think differently.

Our freedom may have been given to us, or may be the results of stoic effort. Whatever we do with it, creates our own success.

Work your own claim

Since visiting some of the world's fascinating and historical mining sites – such as Kalgoorlie in Western Australia, Ballarat in Victoria, Australia, and Crested Butte in Colorado, USA I've often been struck by the relevance of the mining metaphor to our lives. Abraham Lincoln said "The good Lord gives us everything, at the price of an effort." And what a significant effort, and investment of time money and courage, was required from our pioneering prospectors.

When we become clear around what we want our lives to be – at this stage of them, anyway – we need to find that investment of time, money and courage. We need to contribute the price of an effort. Not wanting to waste that effort now, I have great respect for the process of deeply clarifying values, goals and priorities.

When we're first introduced to the practice and pay-offs of goal-setting, it can feel unreal! I really mean unreal - not in the vernacular, but in the literal meaning. Sometimes, we just can't grasp the concrete reality of the process, or the way it actually works.

We are told "Write down your goals" (because they won't come to pass unless they're written down!) and visualise them (because the power of your mind will then automatically lead you in that direction) and affirm them as current reality (because your mind doesn't know the difference between a real and imagined experience).

We nod. We smile. we go along with it. But we're not convinced. It's all a bit hocus pocus, a bit too "magical mystery tour" to be part of our normal routine lives. Sometimes we follow the advice, most often we don't. We attend a seminar or webinar, take notes, download some podcasts, spend a quiet hour or few drawing up some dreams and wishes, perhaps creating a vision board or even a strategic plan ...and the next day get caught up in deadlines and paperwork and family demands and forget it. We haven't got the time.

Nod if you do that. Thank you.

But isn't it infernally annoying when you meet someone who is really getting there, who is reaching success after success, and you ask how, and she tells you it's because she made up her mind to do it? She says she decided it was what she wanted, and she worked out what she had to do to get it and actually went and did those things. Then she tells you she got mentally involved in imagining the whole success trip, and she even started behaving as if she was already there, and amazingly, everything sort of fell into place? Doesn't it make you want to spit?

Because the process works, unfortunately.

I say "unfortunately" because it is an effort. 'It' doesn't actually work at all. We have to. Goal setting, like all other success-oriented activities, requires effort at first, and discipline, before it becomes productive second nature. And like all other habits, it's easier to get started on little things close to home.

I met a great guy some time ago called Chas Tarby, who very successfully established Century 21 Real Estate in Australia. Chas had a simple but strong philosophy for success; one of his tenets was that he doesn't believe in long term goals! Not everyone would agree with this, but it worked for him and his team. They have been, and continue to be, massively successful. Chas maintained that most of us are good on long-term dreams but sometimes not too hot on the action that will take us there. He told me he found that it's worthwhile to habitually set short-term action goals - like a week away - and firmly commit to achieving them. Of course, these short term goals can actually be the interim action steps to achieving the long term dream.

It's an interesting and very workable way of achieving. Because so much has been happening in our world over the last while that the value of long term goal setting has been questioned! Indeed I have shortened all my clients' strategic planning frameworks to a maximum of 5 years – when we used to have 15 and even 20 year time frames.

'...we are designed for flexibility and agility, as long as we are prepared to allow it. '

That's not to say that long term thinking isn't necessary. It is. The longer term Vision is the distant lifestyle or workplace that we are committed to creating. We will be clear on where we are ultimately heading, and what 'terms and conditions' we want to live by. We will hold on to those Values and our Mission or Purpose with continual strength and commitment – or with flexibility if we choose. So they matter.

But the detailed action planning, resource allocation and commitments will be for a much shorter time frame. That's logical. We just can not expect to know what our lives will be like even a month from now. That's fine, we are designed for flexibility and agility, as long as we are prepared to allow it.

In past decades, certainly pre-Covid19, we wanted and expected certainty and control. The lack of it would cause anxiety and even stress. And a lot of people were extremely distressed over the confusion and unpredictability of life. I've been there – not so much with Covid, but over the years of illnesses and events that I have experienced. So I had probably learned the value of trust and surrender long before.

Our lives are enriched when we realise what we can influence and what we can control, releasing what we can't. I am indebted to Stephen Covey for his work in The Seven Habits of Highly Successful People, which introduced the model of our Circle of Influence and Circle of Control. The latter is quite small in fact! But it does exist. I can control my choices, my responses, my reactions, my standards, my values and boundaries. I can control whom I choose to befriend, and who lives in my closest circle of loved ones. It isn't everyone in my family, and I've become OK with that.

When we are 'staking our claim' (which is a reference to the process of early prospectors actually putting wooden stakes in the ground to mark the area they have lodged a claim to work) we are marking out the ground we intend to work in, communicating to ourselves and those in our Circle of Influence where we choose to invest our energy and how we choose our results.

With the changes that the coronavirus has brought to our lives, we need a strong Claim. We need to choose where our next few steps will be placed. We have learned that time is not indefinite, that for many of us it may be limited, and we need to express our love in the present moment. For me, that love is strongly expressed in my work. We will each have our own forms of expression, our own values and boundaries, our own restrictions to overcome. George Bernard Shaw, playwright and thought leader, is famous for saying "Life was not meant to be easy! But it will, my child, be delightful". I'm in for that, are you?

I've often seen people stumped as they sit trying to work out their 5 and 10 year goals. Maybe setting simple clear one-week targets would end up taking them in the right direction automatically, as long as they are aligned with their true life purpose. Ah, that's a big question. Do you know yours?

I've discovered I need to be a big picture thinker. I find if I just focus on the tasks in front of me, I end up busy but not productive. Even if I do all the 'right things' like making my To Do list and focusing on the top five – which was Ivy Lee's legendary advice to Charles Schwab of Bethlehem Steel – I don't necessarily reach my goals.

Unless I've already done the creative thinking around what I really want to achieve, why it matters, and how I might get there. That makes my To Do list meaningful exciting and relevant. I like to devote my day to no more than five tasks these days, as compared to the 20 or so I used to list and ended up feeling a failure at the end of every day! I can focus on five. And I know what Project or Goal those five will serve, so I know I am achieving.

Can I please share a word of warning with you around Achievement?

Back in the days of my sales management career, I learned an invaluable piece of wisdom, from Steve Brown of Fortune Training, in Atlanta Ga. He told us that there were three reasons people fail:

1. They don't know What they are trying to achieve *(and Why it matters! my addition)*.
2. They don't know How to get there.
3. Someone or something gets in the way.

About the How. Everything we know, we know from the Past. True? We have learned it, somehow somewhere, in the days before today.

Do you agree we've seen a lot of change over the last few years? So is there any evidence that what we learned in the Past is exactly what we need to know Now and for the Future?

I can't see any. I believe that all my knowledge could somehow be useful. But there's no guarantee of that. Today is a new day, and it may require new thinking. Does that excite you? Or terrify you? I hope it's the former, but I know a lot of us can fall into fear.

So I recommend, when staking out and planning to work your claim, that you certainly use the knowledge you already have. And – please – stay humble and hungry for more knowledge, because there may well be a better way. So many people are afraid that people will discover they don't know everything. That is exhausting!! Just get it out there, and encourage everyone around you to badge themselves as continuing learners, as students of life.

Many days I find out that my 'how' needs a few adjustments as I go. It could be software, it could be process, it could be health and hygiene management factors. Fortunately I'm flexible! And so are you.

The most exciting aspect of 'claim staking' (or goal setting) is that whatever it takes to achieve what you want is already inside you. I don't believe that anyone has the capacity to seriously set for themselves anything they are not actually

'....whatever it takes to achieve what you want is already inside you.'

capable of achieving. It's already there. It's a matter of using it, with simple but strong commitments.

My clients also tell me that it's not necessarily reaching their goals that is the most rewarding – even if it's a red Ferrari! It's what they learned along the way. And the conditions they have created in their lives as they grew.

Many people say that about entering for Awards for local or national business recognition; whether they win an Award or not, they got to document what they had achieved, and that blew them away! They often say that like many of us, they are always focusing on what they haven't done, rather than what they have. And the entry process forces them to actually recognise their own achievements. Yes!!

It's so easy for us to say we can't, we haven't, we never will, because of external influences, because of our background, our family, our dependents, our self-imposed restrictions. It's also so easy for us to decide to achieve, to develop a plan;, get going and work our plan, and to remain determined and disciplined until we get what we want. The only thing stopping us is us.

A client with whom I really enjoyed working, once sent out a quote to her team "The golden opportunity you are seeking is in yourself. It is not in your environment, it is not in luck or chance or the help of others, it is in yourself alone". I love that.

It's all there, whatever you want, inside you right now. Claim it. It is your stake in the ground. It's who you are. It's your gift to the planet. Your daily success.

Please look where you're going

It was a long long time ago, and beside me in the dual control Volkswagen Beetle was an intrepid driving instructor, who was determined somehow to ensure I would not be a menace to society when I got my driving licence.

We were on our way back from our regular excursion into the wilds of the city traffic. I had indicated correctly, I had negotiated the entry driveway, and I was carefully entering the driving school car park.

Now, let me paint the picture. This car park was square, and held four cars along the rear fence and four cars down each side. Right in the middle were two large wooden posts, side by side, supporting a large sign naming the driving school. I didn't want to hit it, of course, so I held it firmly in my gaze as I entered the square...

'....Look beyond it, at where you want to go.'

"Don't look at it!" he yelled. "Don't look at it, or you'll hit it! Look past it at where you want to go!"

He was right, I would have hit it! With my fixed gaze I was heading right for those looming posts! At the last minute, or so it seems in my memory, I swerved and, now looking where I was going, headed towards the car park corner.

What a lesson! I remember that teacher well - but I bet he doesn't remember the lesson he taught me that day. Many times I catch myself and say "Don't look at it - you'll hit it if you do. Look beyond it, at where you want to go." It's so easy for us to focus on our problems - they're right there in front of us, seemingly impossible to ignore.

At the beach one day with my then Sea Scout son I saw another example; canoes full of little Sea Cubs, trying to manoeuvre a course around a big blue motor boat. "Go around the boat," Akela told them. Why was it that they kept hitting the boat? There was a lot more water around the boat than there was under it! Why? Because they were focusing on the boat, and not on the empty water around it. "The boat! The boat!" their minds cried. It should have been "the water around the boat" or better still, the buoys close by.

And even more importantly, after my first diagnosis of Non-Hodgkin Lymphoma, my beautiful neighbour Pam – who had recently overcome her ovarian cancer diagnosis for the second time – directed me not to focus on this 'bump in the road', but to focus on my life on the other side of the bump. I did, and it worked.

Are there any challenges in your life that are taking your focus away from the desirable end result? Just try not looking at them for a while and looking clearly and firmly at where you want to go - at what you perceive as the most desirable and favourable outcome. If you can do that, you can amazingly see the route to that solution clearly marked out; a route you could never see while you were focused on the problem.

In my experience, it isn't always the exact route you end up taking. Often a better alternative turns up, or you change your mind about the outcome anyway. But it gets you moving, and that's all that matters. Leave behind the depressing paralysis that can arise when problems get bigger than solutions. Just take action. Any action. You'll love yourself for it.

It's not effective, in my experience, to ignore the problem - that's not what I mean. Pushing things underground can often cause even more problems when they eventually pop out again. But looking at it, accepting that it exists, and even better, accepting that dealing with it will be a good learning experience for you - that works.

For many years I worked way too hard, too many long hours, skipping meals or eating them on the run, sitting at my computer until the early hours of the morning. I lived to work – because I loved it. And still do. But I didn't love myself to the same extent.

Fortunately, with my cancer diagnosis, I chose not to allow anyone to tell me what my life span would be. I spent the early part of my life being very compliant with authority – then my freedom to choose took over. Mostly obeying the rules has meant safety and civilisation to me. But occasionally I like to push the boundaries. And this time that was very important. I did hear the words '18 months' but ignored them.

In Australia, the aboriginal people have an ancient practice of 'pointing the bone'. It is a vengeance or punishment ritual of considerable significance. It leaves no trace and never fails to kill its victim. The shape of the killing-bone, or kundela, varies from tribe to tribe. It is deeply sacred, and it will not be written or spoken of.

To me it confirms totally the power of belief and unconscious agreement and acceptance. I was not willing to allow anyone to point the bone at me. I accepted all the healing tools I was prescribed by every trusted authority and practitioner I encountered. I used my own intuition and common sense, and left the polluted air of my beloved home city, and took good time out. I went into remission and my physicians sent my files to the archive.

Yes, a couple of years ago the Lymphoma returned. Quickly diagnosed, and quickly treated. I focused on the 'bump in the road' long enough to get the best advice. I told my haematologist that I wanted to be in remission before my birthday. And I was.

So look past whatever bump is in your road, or any big 'solid' obstruction that's looking up in front of you blocking your view. Peer past it into the distance, at what it will look like when you've overcome your challenge and take it from there.

I've found it's a good idea to never look at where I don't want to go. It's surprisingly easy to get there, unfortunately, if that's where you're looking. It's almost impossible to go smoothly in one direction if you're looking in another, wouldn't you agree?

With any luck, if we keep listening to our driving instructors we just might end up with a licence to drive anywhere we want to! Actually, I'm granting you one now. It has success written all over it.

'...It's almost impossible to go smoothly in one direction if you're looking in another....'

Can you get too much?

A re you getting too much?

Is there any such thing? Can you ever get too much? Bet you'd say no. But of course you don't know what I'm talking about.

If you're sitting reading this book after buying it, I'm pretty sure you're a candidate for this accusation. If you've borrowed if from a friend, like it and want a copy of your own, you're running the risk of becoming one in the future. So perhaps it's timely for me to warn you of the consequences.

I am talking about being a junkie. A self-improvement junkie. A book junkie. A seminar junkie. Have you ever heard anyone accuse you of that - upfront or behind your back? Have you ever asked anyone to accompany you to a seminar or event and had them smile in superior condemnation of anyone who seeks to better their attitude and skills levels? Have you felt guilty because you over-indulged one day on program purchases for your betterment?

We hear it all the time from people! 'I promised my husband I wouldn't buy anything today.' 'My wife will kill me when she knows what I signed up for!'

Well let me reassure you. You can certainly spend too much, if you haven't got it to spend. But you can't get too much information, encouragement, inspiration.

Read everything you can get hold of, written by people who are already where you want to get to. Listen to every intelligent audio program that comes your way that might help you to develop the still leashed potential within you. And go to every seminar and webinar that you instinctively know is right for you to attend. Don't let the doubters put your llfe on limits. Go for what you know will help you.

If your colleagues, family or friends give you advice on your self-development, just check out first that they are where you want to get to.

Only accept advice from those who have clearly achieved the same levels you aspire to. And from the others, be aware with compassion that often, even unconsciously, people can try to hold back their mates from achieving more than them because they do not want to be left behind.

Give them a helping hand up with you. If they don't want to take it, that's their right. Don't let it hold you back.

'....How do you know what's right for you? You just know.......'

How do you know what's right for you? You just know.

Because you've thought through who you want to be, where you want to go, what you want to create in this world, and why it matters.

You mostly know what you know.
You know some of what you don't know.
You don't know most of what you don't know.
But you intuitively know what you want to know.

Trust your knowing.

And please don't confuse the need to keep learning with the fear of not knowing enough or not being good enough.

Here's the paradox. We can never stop learning. It does not matter how well we did yesterday (which was the absolute best we could do, always, given the prevailing circumstances yesterday) – today is a new day with challenges we may never have faced before – and tomorrow is completely unknown. It may be relatively predictable, but not entirely. We have to continue to grow in awareness, knowledge and skill to even survive. To get ahead, to strive, to reach our desired state, we definitely have to keep growing.

As my wise mentor John Nevin once wrote to me on the outside of an envelope "When you're green, you're growing. When you're not, you rot."

I realised then, and I keep getting reminded, that I'm actually growing the most effectively when I do feel green. When I have the courage to say 'I don't know' or 'I wonder how….' And I've discovered it's not age-related!

You can't get too much learning. The brain's unused capacity is well documented, and the mind's sphere of understanding is infinite. I make only one proviso: the work doesn't work if it's without action.

Everything you learn will only work for you if you work for it. Books on shelves, programs in packs and seminar notes unread can't help. We need to take time to review the content

'....the formula doesn't work if it's minus action.'

we scribbled or typed, practise the ideas and information we absorbed, and grow our knowledge skills and beliefs.

Sometimes I hear 'I'm not going to that event, I know all that'. Aaaaargh! I am pretty sure I might have even said it myself! Knowing all that is not enough.

To know and not to do, is not to know. Information and knowledge are separated by experience, by practice, by action. Even as I write these chapters and sections, I have to continually check in to make sure I do know this from real life, from action research, and that I am still learning myself.

There was a time when I was too embarrassed to speak up about the things I didn't know. Terrified to ask a question in class, or in a seminar, in case it revealed the idiot within me. Do you relate?

It undoubtedly held me back for a few years. So many wasted opportunities to learn from some great people around me, because I was afraid of being seen as 'not knowing'.

Many highly qualified professionals suffer through this. Because they are paid for 'knowing', as experts in their field, it is difficult for them to move publicly into learning mode.

My friend John helped me with this too. He modelled humility. Although a hugely successful human being, in business and in life, he was always interested in new information and skills. He never tried to portray himself as someone who had all the answers, although many of us believed he did. Through his influence, I learned early as a leader to stay in enquiry, to welcome being challenged with another point of view. It didn't mean I had to change my mind, or keep it so open all my brains fell out!! I could absolutely hold to my previous decision or perspective, if I felt it was right for me. But I learned it did not diminish me to keep asking questions.

Self-leadership requires a continually growing individual, with an ever-expanding vision, and ever more effective action. That means you can never get enough, let alone too much.

Even if it's only one thing a week, take something new, learn and grow with it. Something from any part of your life – physical, mental, emotional, financial, spiritual. That's success.

Don't waste your energy

Been angry or cross today? Or hurt? Or defensive? How did you find the time?

Or was it a normal human reactive process that arose unbidden and possibly uncontrolled, pushing present events out of your focus so that you relived the past experiences? Bet it was.

Isn't it a fascinating thought? NONE of our negative destructive thoughts and feelings has anything to do with the present moment! Once we realise our life ticks by millisecond by millisecond, it becomes clear that most times what we are thinking and feeling now has nothing to do with now - it's related to something that happened moments ago, or hours or days or even years ago.

What a waste of energy!

It's common knowledge, I think, that we can't change the Past. It's gone, over, finished, "unreal". We can remember, record and learn from it in a clear cognitive process in the present, but we need to know it's the Past.

We can of course change our view of it. As time passes, we often learn new things that give us a new perspective. My sisters and I often discover we each experienced a life event in completely different ways, so we have different points of view. Those experiences are so valuable, because they often take away our self-justification for anger or resentment. That can happen spontaneously – or we can travel in our mind back in time to the event itself and choose to see what we learned and for what we are grateful. That's good work, if you have a good facilitator.

Similarly with the future. In this present time, we can have goals, make plans, assess probabilities and imagine possibilities. In fact that is a wonderful way to Stake our Claim and work our action plans. But we can't live in the time to come - it will always be "unreal". True?

I don't know if this is true for you, but many of us forget to live in the Present. Our busy minds race back and forth between one and the other, like the "fast forward" and reverse" buttons, without taking time to listen to "play" in the Present. Because we're human.

What's the right button, the one that cuts the other two and brings reality into focus?

The answer is awareness. Constantly being able to remind ourselves that this is the Present, the Past has gone. So all our reactions are a waste of time and energy. We have all made Past choices. We can celebrate them or we can let them go. And make Present choices from awareness.

There is a lot that goes on around us that we can't control. But one thing we can is what goes on in our own heads - with practice!

'....There is one thing over which each person has absolute inherent control and that is his mental attitude.'

W Clement Stone said "there is one thing over which each person has absolute inherent control and that is his mental attitude".

It's also his/her thought processes, and feelings, once they are realised.

Sometimes "staged" anger or another particular controlled emotion is of value in a constructive way. Occasionally it's important for someone to understand how deeply we feel about an event or a condition, to impact or influence how we move forward together. It's the "present moment" control that makes the difference. The uncontrolled reactive emotions like anger, pride, jealousy, hatred, envy, etc are what gobble up our precious time and energy resources. Just as it's a waste of time and energy to sit there thinking of a past and long healed physical injury, isn't it useless to treat a mental or emotional scar that way too?

A few years ago I had a number of really bad experiences. Illness, at every level. Physical debilitation and continual pain. Heavy medication, surgery, and the side effects of all of that. The tragic death of a longed for grand-daughter, and the ghastly pain of my son as he lived through it. Financial stress unlike anything I had ever experienced. The loss of friends and family. I was in the Pit, the lowest level of my Emotional Energy Spectrum.

Eventually, as we do when we have courage, I found my way back. To real friends, to valuable work, to a presence of mind. To self-love, self-nurturing, self-awareness.

But for a long time, while I was on that recovery path, I still kept looking back. Until one day over coffee, a generous and wise friend patiently listened to my pain. When I had – eventually – finished, he said: "That is one of the saddest stories I have ever heard in my life. And I never ever want to hear it again. Let it go. It's past. Live now."

It took a while. I did find myself re-telling my sad story, for another year or so. I think it was my version of an excuse, or explanation, for the changes people might see in me.

Another friend, a wonderful coach, reminded me not to refer to 'my' illness She explained that I was simply reinforcing my identity as a sick person. I knew she was right. And as you know, knowing and doing often have a time lag in between. I stuck it out, and now I can not remember what it felt like to feel so sorry for myself.

It is simply common sense to realise that the feelings we hold when we approach a task or a goal will have a major impact on the outcome. So letting go of any grief, anger or fear from the past is essential, if we want to bring hope, courage and confidence to our current activities.

'....the feelings we hold when we approach a task or a goal will have a major impact on the outcome. '

Have you noticed that some people just don't want to let go? It almost seems that they enjoy the sympathy, the attention, the admiration for their heroism. The pity, even. Aaaargh!!! Perhaps that was me too!!!

At some point, if we are lucky (and smart), we get to realise that the payoff for the sad story is not enough. We want more from life than pity. At that point we know it's time to sit quietly. Write it out, if that helps. Put the sad story gently and respectfully into an envelope or a box, if it is in hard copy. Or mentally into a beautifully wrapped package, or balloon. We can take it to the edge of the sea, burn it and scatter the ashes, as I did. Or we can allow the package, the balloon, the story, to float higher and higher, into the stratosphere. We can even allow it to send some gold dust back to us, as a reminder of the gifts of strength and wisdom it has created for us.

The path of least resistance, the path using the least energy, is the one with no constraints. No beliefs holding us back, no anger grief or guilt, nothing but learning and gratitude.

I met a beautiful young man who was described to me as an angel. He suffered from epilepsy as a child, and had completely lost his short term memory. He had the calmest, most serene temperament I had ever encountered. He simply lived entirely in the Present, and found no reason there to be irritable or fearful. He was loving, and he was loved.

A proactive mind - alert, open and non-judgemental, with a clear view ahead, is energy conservation in its purest form. What magnificent companions and colleagues we are when we have the presence to listen without judgement or conceit, to speak without fear and to serve each other with complete focus and full powered commitment.

Save energy and get into the present now!

Time waits for no one...

Time fascinates me. I'm convinced it's an illusion. How one hour can go past in a flash and another seemingly take forever, only serves to persuade me that whatever time is, it changes. An Australian poet, Ian Mayleston Mudie, said it well:

> *"We see time pass, yet know not if our visions live in the past or future. All we know is that a sunlit dream moves fast or slow."*

Another quote I like: 'Yesterday's history - tomorrow's a mystery — today is a gift – that's why it's called the present.'

At the risk of being repetitive, I know that now is all there is. Life moves millisecond by millisecond, and the only point of power is in the absolute present. In fact, in that present there is unlimited power and energy, it seems to me. it's just the lack of focus that weakens it. We hang on tight to experiences that are just-gone or long-gone, or we daydream and imagine about the times to come. When all the while it's what is happening NOW that's really happening. Life is not happening yesterday - let go of whatever did. It is unreal. Life is not happening tomorrow - it's only a dream time, it is unreal. Now is the only real there is.

Benjamin Franklin admonished, "If you love life, don't squander time".

What are the burglars and housebreakers of time - the habits that we let steal our powerful present and throw it away on the past and never-to-be tomorrow?

- How about apathy? A "who cares" view, an "it'll do" outlook, robs us of the power to achieve our best, and be of the most highly rewarded value. I learned that a rut and a grave are the same — it's only the dimensions that are different. When we resign ourselves to past conditions, without gifting ourselves the power of change, we have died to our potential, to the gifts we could actually bring to our world.
- Pride is another - the insecure stubbornness that won't allow us to admit we're wrong or to alter our course. That is very costly, hugely expensive. It's been called one of the 'Seven Deadly Sins' for a good reason. It separates us, it assumes others will find us unworthy, so we have to show them how inferior they are. Such delusion. Such pain.
- Anger is a serious thief. If it's there for more than 15 seconds, Elizabeth Kubler Ross told us, it isn't a current annoyance, it's unfinished business from the past. Finish it or let it go. Some anger is justified and must be acted on. The 15 second rule is a good one. Feel it, do something and let it go. Bringing it back up is like food poisoning, damaging to our own system and extremely unpleasant for others.
- Guilt - what a waster! Realising you've done something you could have done better may be helpful. So you can amend it. Do it again. Fix it. Then let go! You've read that I won't have 'shoulds' in my life. Shoulds are designed to impose guilt. It's a dirty sandpit, which lots of people like to play in, and tell you that you 'should'..... Don't go near it. You're too precious, and your energy matters.

113

- Not being You! Have you noticed how much time and energy our masks and roles take to keep up? Trying to please others, and being what they want us to be instead of what we are, just can't happen in the present - we literally have to use past and future to check ourselves out if we're playing these games. In the Present, you are only you. You don't know how to be anything else. And – wanting to be like somebody else is wasting the person you already are. If you need to be told how precious you are, just as you are, let me know! What you are doing as You may not always be living up to your Magnificence – but you have choice and control around that.

- Lack of forgiveness of others, holding grudges, remembering past hurts - the pain remembered from an old injury is often much worse than that originally felt! I've been reminded of that only this week. I have no right to hold old anger. My judgement is tiring. It's so liberating to release it. I can still choose who I want to hang out with, but I can be neutral around those I release. They have been generous with their lessons around my values and boundaries.

- Lack of forgiveness of yourself - the mental torture we go through again and again reliving old mistakes and foolishness. Let yourself make errors, grow through them without nagging - give yourself the same courtesy you would give others. Mistakes truly are the only way we learn, and yours and mine demonstrate such courage and commitment to living fully. We honour our errors. They have made us wise.

'...Let yourself make errors, grow through them....give yourself the same courtesy you would others.'

- Lack of planning or direction - if you care enough to want to live each moment fully, spend a moment or two consciously planning how. Teach your children how to choose and plan. Review, choose and plan again. Direction is big picture, planning is detail. You'll need both. Some of us want direction first, others need to plan today before they can check direction. Not right or wrong, better or worse, just different. Know yourself and how you live best.
- Indecision is mental paralysis. Strong goals and values help make decisions easier. Everything comes to those who wait – maybe? - but faster to those who don't! Yes, there is a right time – but you won't know it until you move through indecision. If you really can't make a decision, toss a coin. You'll know what side you want to turn up.

So what are the Dos, the "life creators", the behaviour patterns that make moments glow with excitement and achievement?

- Love. Enough to let others be what they need and want to be as best they can, and do the same for yourself. Loving like this can't be done in the past or the future, only in the present.
- Give yourself space to think, to re-focus into the present, to relax and be still so the world comes back into perspective and the "dark river of time" stops rushing past. Even five minutes will allow your peace. One minute in a workshop centres everyone. And you will want to make it a habit, because it feels good, and makes life easier.
- Discern your priorities. My dad used to jokingly say "never put off till tomorrow what you can do the day after". Not! Know what needs to be done and what doesn't, and what is the best use of that precious present moment. And if all else fails, remember the Ironing Basket theory.
- Allow, don't criticise. Everyone's perception is their reality, and it will most often be different from everyone else's. Time

115

is INVESTED on improving ourselves, but time is WASTED on disapproving of others or trying to improve them, unless they have asked you to.

- Be the Master of the life you lead, not the victim. Choose each act, each moment consciously. Take responsibility, rather than "copping out" and blaming everybody else. And don't let anyone, especially me, direct your choices. My words are offered as ideas and suggestions, not as controlling directions. There is no one right way.

'....In our true reality, we must be self-reliant. '

Yesterday is experience. Tomorrow is hope. For many of us, today is just getting from one to the other. How sad that is, just marking time, just getting through. Waiting. What a waste of a lifetime.

In the now, there is only you. In our true reality, we must be self-reliant. Some years ago I found a poem called 'Comes the Dawn' by an unknown author, which says it all:

"After a while you learn the subtle difference
Between holding a hand and chaining a soul,
And you learn that love doesn't mean leaning
And company doesn't mean security,
And you begin to learn that kisses aren't contracts
And presents aren't promises,
And you begin to accept your defeats
With you head up and your eyes open,
And learn to build all roads
on today because tomorrow's ground
Is too uncertain for plans, and futures have
A way of falling down in mid-flight.

After a while you learn that even sunshine
Burns if you get too much
So you plant your own garden and decorate
Your own soul, instead of waiting
For someone to bring you flowers.
And you learn that you really can endure...
That you really are strong
And you really do have worth.
And you learn and learn...
With every goodbye you learn."

What are you hanging on to from the past that you could grow better without? What do you need to say goodbye to?

Please learn every day to do your best in the present minute, in the present second. You never actually can do your best it seems, but every second you get better at it.

You cannot make the most of the moment too soon, because the next moment it is too late. And everything you do will be successful.

The answer is probably action!

Wouldn't it be fun to do something right now that everyone tells you not to do? Just for the joy of it? Actually, it's something that could be quite useful. So don't get too excited.

You know how everybody tells you to think positively, and to treat each problem as an opportunity, and never ever to dwell on your problems or focus on them?

Well, I am going to suggest you do just that, just for a while. Let's dig out the problems. Really get into them.

I'd like you to write them down. All the things that are wrong in your life. All the work hassles you have, all the relationship problems, starting with the big ones that float on the top and then delving right down to the bottom and bringing up all the little nit-picky ones. Every single problem you can think of. All the things you complain about to yourself, even if you don't to anyone else.

Make a list. On a big sheet of paper. Or several!

And keep writing all the way until you know you are empty. There just isn't any problem left in your life that you haven't written down. Keep asking - is that it? Keep going until you can say "Yes, I have no more problems".

Massive! Well done!

Now – the next step – beside each one, write down the reason these problems exist. And they have to be reasons from within YOU, not external reasons. That's the only rule of the game, you can't blame anyone else.

Some of the reasons I can think of for some of mine are:

- fear (of all sorts of different things, including earning too much, being judged adversely, making mistakes, etc etc)
- laziness or pleasure addiction (something more enjoyable to do)
- confused objectives
- lack of commitment
- trying to please others
- being unwilling to pay the price.

But you've got to be very careful. Because for me, anyway, it's very easy to get hooked into the mind games, working out the rationale, the logic, the causes, and even perhaps the excuses. And that is not where the solutions to the problems lie.

So when you've written down the reason for each of these problems in your life, write down what you could do about it.

Be honest. There is always something you could do. You might not like the idea, but write it down anyway. If there is a number of things you could do, write them all down.

'...it's very easy to get hooked into the mind games, working out the rationale, the logic, the causes and even perhaps the excuses.'

Catherine Palin-Brinkworth

Now look back over your list. Look at the causes within you, and look at the choices you could now make to do something about it.

Make one choice, and write it down. 'I will…..' 'I am going to……..' Put a date – even a time – next to the action. Be real. Don't overcommit so you sabotage yourself. Allow yourself the time and energy to complete each action. But don't stop. Keep going until every single problem has an internal cause, a possible solution and a decision and commitment. How long will it take? It doesn't matter. It only matters that you do it. And you may even find that once a few have been cleared away, the others also disappear.

Now let's be daring again. There may be some problems you have, that you are actually quite attached to. For instance, I remember once realising that I couldn't break up with my life partner because then I'd have nothing to complain about! So you have my absolute permission to choose, decide and commit to keeping the problem. But now you will know that you have chosen it, and you will never be able to honestly complain about it again.

There isn't one problem I can think of that can't be solved by actually DOING something about it. Even it it's not the perfect action, the absolute optimum, it's good enough. Every step towards a solution is a step in the right direction.

I know. You want to argue with me. You want to say that your problems are different. They might be a physical difficulty that can't be overcome. They might be a life circumstance that simply won't change in the short term. I really have heard it all.

And here's the way it is. Your solution might be to see it differently. To change your perspective. To learn new 'management' skills. To review your feelings and preferences about a situation.

For instance, I have heard people say 'I have to go to work.' No, they don't. Many people don't, and somehow they survive. Or 'I have to look after my kids.' Actually, they don't. Many people don't. I applaud the values they hold that have them think that is a requirement, and I support them completely. But the reality is that they don't have to do anything, except breathe. There is always a choice, a decision, a commitment. You do have a great deal of personal power.

'....The emotions and mental barriers won't go away by themselves. '

You know yourself how to solve each and every problem you have. You also know why you are not already doing what you need to do to solve them. The emotions and mental barriers won't go away by themselves. They need a repellent.

The answer is action. Just do it.

I remember a very lively and lovely guy who used to wind up meetings with great gusto and the exhortation:

"Remember that all of these thoughts and all of these words mean nothing. They mean absolutely nothing. Unless YOU put them into action. ACTION. A C T I O N !!!" (at full volume!)

o   Action such as apologising for an error or a misunderstanding.
o   Action like going for a short walk every hour of daylight.
o   Action like thinking and writing in your journal so you can map out your future actions and choose in the present.
o   Action like calling someone you care about, just to let them know.
o   Action like decluttering your desk or your home.
o   Action like hiring a coach or mentor to help you for a while.

- o Action like going to your local yoga class, or gym, because it feels good.
- o Action like drinking another glass of water.
- o Action like looking in the mirror and approving of yourself.

If you've been a person who is critical of others, you may find yourself criticising these possible actions (or me for suggesting them!) That's OK, notice it and let it go. And choose an action you do want to take, towards your life vision.

For some time it has been a focus for people to determine their life's purpose. Some of my colleagues run seminars for that outcome, others are coaches or mentors who can support the process.

I don't think it matters. Really.

30+ years ago, after a healthy career in management and business development, I started my own consulting business. My graphic designer asked me about the purpose of my business. Good question! I told him that it was to help people discover their own magnificence. Because when they got that, their capabilities multiplied, they treated customers and colleagues with more respect, and their business flourished.

His response was interesting. He said 'You can't tell people that! They won't hire you. Business owners have a vested interest in people NOT knowing their own magnificence – then they can pay them less'.

Interesting. It was 3 decades ago, and I knew he was right. He went on…

'You have to build a Trojan Horse. Like sales or leadership training. So you can get through the gates (get booked) and then help people discover how magnificent they are.'

So I did. I eventually built a training organisation, using the practical processes I'd learned through my career. They were very well received, yet I don't think anyone realised why they worked so well, or how we had delivered the core message.

A few years in, I realised that we do teach that which we most want to learn. I found difficulty in accepting my own magnificence. Even now, it goes against all the modesty my mother taught me, to put that in writing!

Now that my generation has done such a good job and raised our children with healthy self-esteem – for the most part – my life purpose has changed. And I'm not telling you what it is. Yet.

How did I know? I simply thought about what really mattered to me. What had kept my energy high, continually learning, overcoming every obstacle.

If you don't know your life purpose – keep breathing anyway. Your presence on this planet is valuable, even if you don't realise it. I know you will have given a great deal already, and you have much more to contribute. Your happiness and joy help to raise our energy systems, and you matter.

Just keep taking the action that inspires you, that rewards you, that you know has helped others. That's success.

5

WHERE TO NOW?

*For each one of us it's different. Our own unique talents and abilities create a
different path and direction for us. Perhaps unlike that of anyone else we know.
We will get what we expect. We will go where we point ourselves. We will be what
we know our selves to be. We can be all that we can be. And that is success.*

Who dares wins!

When my sisters and I were children, the word "dare" figured fairly frequently in our vocabulary. "I dare you!" was all the challenge we needed to get us going on some particular stunt or feat. "Bet you don't dare!" was enough for us to have to prove we could, and did! Admittedly I was the older, bossy and challenging playmate; thank heavens the others survived.

I remember there was actually a game of "Dare" which went around for a while at school, with each of us becoming in turn braver and more foolhardy as we challenged each other to try crazier stunts - and all this was in a private girls' only high school! Goodness knows what happened in the real world.

One day someone got hurt. They usually do. The bubble burst. the game was banned, and we all meekly and submissively went back into our well-behaved little shells. The Principal had spoken. "Daring" was forbidden. Why? Because it was risky, because you could get hurt, because those in authority wanted you to do what they wanted you to do, so that they knew where you were and could control you.

In hindsight, they were doing their best to keep us safe. I'm not decrying their efforts and intentions - they had only our wellbeing at heart. But do you wonder how any of us got to be entrepreneurs? Is it any surprise that most of our top performers in business and in sport over the decades have come from a relatively hardier background than a protective private school, where who dared won, and that was the way it worked!

Those of us with more "privileged" backgrounds – and many of us have moved into that description now with our own children – just might have had the daring choked out of us. Until we found it again.

Watch your children, and the young people around you, and encourage them to dare! Because on that daring rests their success and the success of the world.

Not of course without respect for human life and limb, especially their own. And not without the proper regard for other's rights of all kinds. But with guts and courage to test themselves against the upper limit of their capacity and endurance. And dare yourself too.

Sure you can get hurt. But we're mendable. As Margery Williams tells us in the Velveteen Rabbit, you don't get real until you've lost a few whiskers and rubbed off a bit of fur. 'Getting real doesn't happen to people who have sharp edges, or are easily broken,' she says. And it takes a few tests, a few dares, to see how many risks you're capable of taking and getting right back up there again.

> ' ....Sure you can get hurt. But we're mendable.... '

I remember a motivational speaker early in my management career. "Close your eyes and stretch high on your toes until you can go no further" she said. So we did. We couldn't go any further. "Now take a deep breath and find two more inches". And we did find them. Every one. It was amazing.

Stop reading and think of one thing you're working on right now. Imagine yourself doing it to the absolute limit of your capacity. Now take a deep breath and stretch two inches more – or five centimetres. See yourself doing it even better, way beyond what you previously imagined possible. Now do it.

Can you think of something you have been avoiding, or procrastinating over? I don't mean waiting for the right time, as I did with this book. I mean you know it's the right time, and you're freaking out. Just make a mental note of it.

Now cut your mind. Maybe close your eyes, envisage a clean white screen in front of you, without an image or words. Now imagine what your life will be like when it is done. It's your fantasy – you can make it as fabulous as you want! Anything beyond now is pure imagination, just ignore any probabilities your logical mind wants to give you. Turn the brightness up, the colours, the contrast. Enlarge the image. Now inject feelings on to the image, and turn it from a still to a movie. I dare you.

In your movie, notice a calendar somewhere in the picture. Does it have a date on it? Create one. Feel the joy, the celebration, the absolute delight of completion. Make it real. Now open your eyes, and make it real.

Please don't worry if you weren't able to do that – obviously you had to read it through first and then remember what to do. It's not always easy. But if you start, it will get easier, I promise. And it's worth it.

Often our best and highest choices will be scary. (If they are comfortable, they're not big enough). So this is a great exercise to do, to believe in the value of your dreams, to get you out of inaction. I've used it with this book!

Dare means to have the necessary courage or

'...Often our best and highest choices will be scary....'

127

boldness for something. There have been times when I have needed to find that courage to get out of bed! And if my teachers at high school called a girl 'bold' that was the ultimate in condemnation. So we all have a bit of 'stuff' going against us from time to time. It's called life. Fortunately we have each other, and it's now so much easier to find our support network, anywhere in the world.

"Who Dares Wins" is actually the motto for the British Army's elite Special Air Service (SAS). A 1982 movie featured a daring – and successful - escape plan. It has also been used for game show titles. Clearly it's a great inspirational phrase.

If it works for you – that's all that matters. If you need someone to 'dare' you to be successful – I'll do that! Just choose your goal, and take a risk. I know you'll smash it.

Are you sure you want to be wealthy?

E veryone knows how much fun it is to give. Whether it is knowledge you are sharing, donations you make, gifts to something or someone important to you, it is a really good feeling. You feel that the effort you have put into creating your assets becomes really worthwhile when you get to share it with someone else. Of all the people I think I have ever spoken to about their purpose in life, I don't think anyone has ever said they want to succeed for their own sake. It is always for someone else's.

Ever tried to pour water out of an empty bucket?

Ever wanted to buy something for someone and not had the money? Ever felt deeply that you wanted to give support to a cause and not been able to afford it? Ever wanted to help someone out of a simple misery and not been able to think of a way? Doesn't it hurt?

Because you can't give unless you've got.

It's as simple as that. You can be as caring and generous as you like, but unless you have something tangible to give, whether it's cash or goods or knowledge, or your time, you are of limited help. So isn't it in everyone's interest for you to be as wealthy as possible?

Before those of you reared in a self-denial ethic turn the page – or throw this book away - just think about it.

> *'....People can create and trade goods without limit. That's exciting.'*

The wonderful Bob Proctor says all of us were born the same - we were all born rich. Some of us set about getting rid of that wealth as fast as we can - for some ridiculous reason we seem to think we don't deserve it! Buckminster Fuller told us that money growth is UNLIMITED. There is enough money for five billion human beings to be millionaires. People can create and trade goods without limit. That's exciting.

You don't have to take from anyone else to create your own wealth. And you don't have to do anything immoral or illegal. In fact, if you do you'll destroy it. It's all there for the asking.

Poverty is a horrible aspect. If you are poor in spirit, how can you possibly help others to be strong? If it is holy and worthwhile for all of us to abandon our worldly goods how could we share any? Give away all you have, and there is nothing left to give! It's all gone! The secret is to give some, save some, make it grow, give more, make more - and have more to give. It applies to tangible and intangible assets. It is in everyone's interests for you to be wealthy.

Put a value on your labour - on your time, on your knowledge and on your own unique temperament that makes it all work. Do you want that to be a low value? If it were of little value, who would want it? Price yourself high. According to the law of supply and demand, it should be high - there is only one of you! And be worth it.

So many of us have a fear of success. We are embarrassed about the praise and recognition we get when we succeed. When I was at school, it was a desirable attribute to be mediocre. To succeed would have been a disaster. Good, if it was sport. But really bad if you were the 'brainbox' or nerdy. So that carries over to our adult life, and is one heap of a burden to throw off. We often get just as embarrassed about the physical pleasures success can bring. I know I spent a lot of time apologising for my prestige car and explaining my designer clothes away. Weird, huh? Unless you got it by foul means, love it and be proud of it - it is a reflection of your value.

As you've probably heard, it is not money which is the root of all evil, it is the love of money for it's own sake which causes pain. That sort of greed, the grabbing and the grasping, is the cause of unlimited suffering.

But the fruits of hard labour, and of knowledge and skills hard-won, could not ever be the root of all evil.

It is so good to be able to organise special times for friends, so much fun to give generously to charities and causes. And you can't do it unless you've got plenty.

The more you give, the more somehow you get; some call it the Law of Karma. Everything you put out seems to return ten-fold. Try it! My teacher guided me to give 10% - and to grow the 100% so the gift kept getting bigger.

'....the fruits of hard labour, and of knowledge and skills hard-won, could not ever be the root of all evil.'

131

Catherine Palin-Brinkworth

But remember, it is hard to practise charity when one is poor.

It is hard to share experience and knowledge if you don't have the time and freedom. It is hard to share love when you are not filled with it. It is hard to feed anyone else when you're starving yourself.

Think how much good you can do for the rest of the world with your wealth and plenty!

Although the coronavirus created world-wide chaos and financial trauma, many of us in the western world are still so incredibly privileged. We have somewhere to live, plenty to eat and drink and in the main, we are able to earn enough to live on. I think we sometimes take that for granted – yet we are so much better off than so many billions of people on our planet.

It's worth thinking about how wealthy we already are. More attracts more, and yes we can afford to share.

I wish you great riches.

A lesson from sculpture

B ack in the days when I only had one surname, I coined Palin's Law of Behavioural Dynamics. "People will generally behave the way you expect them to behave."

I was newly promoted into a sales management role, I was studying psychology, and I was fascinated by behavioural 'Laws'. So I decided to have one. No, seriously, I was fascinated by human performance and the predictors of it.

We were using a widely respected selection tool at the time, and we relied on it for recruitment. I referenced it for my management and coaching strategies with individual salespeople. It was helpful. But not as helpful as my Law.

Over the years that Law has proven to be a reliable guide. Sure, there were the occasional exceptions that took me by surprise. But by and large it held good. If I treated people with respect and courtesy, with an expectation they would reciprocate, they did. If I mistrusted them, believed they would let me down or fail in their efforts - they must have read my mind, or at least my face or voice.

Somehow they seemed to know what I really thought of them – and they made sure they lived up to it. Does any of this sound familiar to you? With anyone - say with your children?

With ongoing research, I discovered that someone was there before me! The psychological theory known as the "Pygmalion Effect" is actually well documented. It is valid in management, sales, education and training; in fact in every conceivable human relationship. It's fascinating, when you observe with awareness.

In Greek mythology, Pygmalion was a sculptor who carved a statue of a beautiful woman. He loved her deeply and imagined her alive. The gods took pity on him and she was brought to life. The sculptor actually made her become his creation fulfilled, by the power of his goals dreams and wishes.

The fable was used a few thousand years later by George Bernard Shaw in his play Pygmalion, on which the 1960's hit musical 'My Fair Lady' is based.

In the original play, Eliza Doolittle explains to Colonel Pickering, the friend of her mentor:

"You see, really and truly, apart from the things anyone can pick up (the dressing and the proper way of speaking and so on) the difference between a lady and a flower girl is not how she behaves but how she is treated. I shall always be a flower girl to Professor Higgins because he always treats me as a flower girl and always will".

She said it all. We are all like Eliza. We behave according to the way we are treated. We do our best, often unconsciously, to live up to other's expectations of us - bad or good! It's as if our identity is partly formed by others and their opinion of us. Could that be true for you?

Scientists have tested it with rats.

Robert Rosenthal worked with KL Fode in 1963. They required two groups of students to test some laboratory rats for 'maze capability'. They told the first group that the rats were especially bred to be 'maze bright'. And they told the second group of students that the rats were especially 'maze dull'. The results of the studies were conclusive – and completely supported the stories that each group had been told. In reality, they were all standard lab rats and not specially bred one way or the other. The students unconsciously influenced the performance of the rats in order to fit the expected results. It's called the 'experimenter expectancy' effect. Or Pygmalion.

I remember when I first discovered Rosenthal's work. It dazzled me. And it appalled me.

Because they've tested it - more sadly - with school students.

Rosenthal went on to run another study with Lenore Jacobsen the same year, at an elementary school just south of San Francisco. He wanted to see if the same effect would occur with teachers and students.

In the experiment, all the students in a class were given a standard IQ test. After the results were scored, the researchers informed the teachers that five students in the class had unusually high IQ scores and would probably be "spurters" who leaped ahead of their classmates during the remainder of the year. In reality, these five children were picked at random! By the end of the year, all the children had gained in IQ, but the five "spurters" had gained much more than other students.

Evidently the teachers treated them differently, after being told to expect sudden improvement.

And we test it every day with our clients, customers and colleagues. Perhaps even our children and other family members and friends. They do what we unconsciously expect of them.

A surprising finding was that when some of the other children in the control group gained in IQ, they were judged and treated unfavourably by their teachers! They obviously did not like it when anyone did not act predictably. (Ouch. Do you ever get cross when people behave unexpectedly?)

So the question has to be asked – how can I use this to be productive and helpful?

The answer is positive expectation.

> **' ....The answer is positive expectation. '**

The very best service providers I have ever seen, work this way. Some of them call it "the assumed close". I know it's Pygmalion in action. They know their prospective customers are customers already and treat them that way before the sale is made. They know their customers will be long term precious relationships for them, sources of referrals and recommendations; and they treat them that way from minute one.

I have seen others, tentative and diffident, nervous of being persuasive in case they were thought pushy, and backing away from asking for the order in case the prospects thought they were "selling".

Their fear created exactly what they feared. They weren't selling, were they? And therefore the prospective customer couldn't buy, could she? Another expectation met.

But more importantly perhaps, their fear shows in the most unconscious of behaviours. Body language and vocal inflexions are the biggest giveaways of emotion in any communication. So with their own negative program impacting on their prospective customer, of course they will say no. Who wouldn't?

We've been told by wise guides in books, videos and in person, that the way to get what we want is to behave as if we already have it. So it is with Pygmalion. To be what you want, act as if you already are, and of course then, you are! Others around you will automatically respond appropriately - it's inevitable.

It is not a good idea to give praise undeservedly, or to pursue any other insincere or false path of persuasion with our colleagues or customers. Yet I remember with delight a thought shared by a very young colleague: "A person may not be as good as you tell them but they'll try hard afterwards!"

Have a go at creating the world you want to live and work in for yourself, with your words and deeds, and with your mental expectations too.

Form positive expectations of the people you want to work and live with. And be prepared and excited when someone acts more positively than you had expected.

Wishing you successful sculpting!

> '.... A person may not be as good as you tell them but they'll try hard afterwards!'

Green, growing and absolutely alive

One time I was asked to run a training session for the incoming voluntary leaders of a business networking group. It was to be one of those deep and meaningful sessions, to really help them think through the "why's" of building and running their local groups successfully, as well as the "how's".

It seemed prudent for me to stop and think through my own "why's" about the reasons I had first become involved (against much temptation not to, I might add). Because I know that we do an immeasurably better job at anything with far greater commitment and a far, far higher chance of excelling, if we know the reason for doing it, the real purpose behind the exercise. Isn't it curious how "why's" sound like "wise"?

So I looked at my own reasons for belonging to, and supporting, this organisation. The reason for me was GROWTH. In many areas.

My own, for one.

Most of us operate, whether we admit it or not, from the "what's in it for me?" point of view. I needed help, encouragement, and sheer practical how-to tuition, which I got. As I became more involved, I saw more GROWTH. I saw the growth of the organisation and its reach, and through it the growth of many successful small and not-so-small businesses. And through them the growth of their community, and possibly even the growth of our state and national economy and the evolution of the planet.

A wonderful member, the incomparable businesswoman Jeannie Pratt, shared a thought at one meeting that I later learned was coined by Dr Robert Schuller - 'Bloom Where You Are Planted'! The phrase inspired me - and turned into a successful platform presentation.

'....Bloom where you are planted....'

That presentation focuses on what I had learned about growth. It has been given to businesspeople all over the world. I've been asked for it by community groups, service clubs, franchise groups and industry associations. These days it's often called Get up and Grow.

Part of it is a formula. A simple mnemonic for the word GROWTH, which helps to remind me of what works when you make that awesome decision that you want to be better than you are currently managing to be. Here it is, with my thanks to John Nevin for his help in developing it:

G is for generosity. Don't hesitate to give, of your time, your warmth, your wisdom, your experiences. All of your lessons, which by now you take for granted, can so often help others through their time of growth. The more you give, the more you will be astounded at how much you get back; that's not why you do it, but it's an amazing side effect. Be a giver, in all aspects of your life. You will never be drained, I guarantee it. I also know that when I've stopped giving, out of fear that there wouldn't be enough, the well dried up.

R is for responsibilities. Take them on unhesitatingly, without fear.

You will find the resources you need to live up to them. Each new responsibility brings new growth. And take responsibility for your own life – know that no-one can make you think, feel or do anything, you are in absolute control of your own thoughts, you can't blame anyone or anything for your life – and you don't have to give them the credit either!

O is for an open mind. The world is a classroom full of teachers, and everyone has something of wisdom to share with us. It is our responsibility to find out what that is. You can't learn anything and therefore can't grow, with a closed mind. Be careful of criticism, even when it is called "constructive", because it closes minds, faster than anything else.

W is for wisdom. Developing a sense of discernment which enables you to know what is appropriate and what not, and when. It keeps balance in your growth, and will prevent your generosity and all those new responsibilities from blowing your life out. It's the healthy factor that keeps balance in all things. Knowledge is not wisdom. The most constructive use of knowledge goes a way towards it. But it's the ability to think independently, to weigh ideas up against your values, to assess impact and choose carefully, that contribute most.

T is for trust. Trust in the universe, or God, whatever is your Faith. Because everything always does happen for a reason, and everything always turns out just as it is meant to, although sometimes for the life of you, you can't see it. You can never make a wrong decision – everywhere leads you somewhere you were meant to be.

Trust in others – Palin's Law Of Behavioural Dynamics says that people will behave as you expect them to – well, 99% of the time. Because when you expect someone to behave in a certain way, you treat them as if they already have, and they can't help but live up to it, bad or good.

Trust in yourself, because you are intrinsically perfect, with all the wisdom and knowledge you need to handle any situation you find yourself in. You're just on a growth path, and all the mistakes you make are a big wonderful perfect learning curve.

H is for honour. It's the most important one of all, because without honour there is nothing. People of honour are not just the ones who do not lie, cheat or steal; they're the ones who always do what they say they will do. I'm so sad that selling, business and entrepreneurship has too often come into question because of a past lack of honour by someone we don't even know. We have a right to the highest level of respect, and the only way to get it is for each one of us to live indisputably, continually, a life of honour. It's up to us.

Honour and respect your family, your company, your colleagues and most of all yourself. You deserve it.

You are growing.

In all the years I knew my magnificent mentor, John Nevin, he sent me many items in the mail. I learned early never to discard the envelope without checking it carefully. Often there were wise words scribbled on it somewhere!

One time when I was new in my own business, I received another envelope with writing all around its border. This one read 'When you're green, you're growing. When you're not, you rot." (I think I've told you that before.)

Growing means you don't know where you

'....Growing means you don't know where you are.'

are. You don't know what you're doing. If you did, you wouldn't be growing. Of course you're green. Possibly to the gills.

Growing isn't comfortable. As Disney Muppet, Kermit the Frog says "It's not easy being green!" But it's absolutely essential. I think it's why we're here.

Success means growth.

First Footing – it's New Year's Day

Every New Year brings another wonderfully exciting opportunity to unleash our ever expanding potential upon an unsuspecting and possibly unready world. What a thought! Can you handle it?

First-Footing is a Scots custom of Hogmanay, or New Year – it means the visiting of friends and family immediately after midnight and often sees a Scotsman rushing from house to house. The First-Foot in the house traditionally is supposed to be a dark, handsome male carrying a piece of coal, whisky, Scottish shortbread and black bun - a rich dark fruitcake encased in pastry. The visitor in return is given a small glass of whisky. I always thought it was extremely unfair that it couldn't be a dark-haired young woman – or these days, an older one.

Do you set your New Year goals? It always seems the perfect time to review and revise, to examine past efforts, evaluate the methods used and results achieved from them, and to free wheel the mind on to new challenges and adventures. It seems compulsory on New Year's Eve to glance back and take credit for the achievements of the previous twelve months, with appreciation for the help given and the lessons learned. Then to turn and face the year ahead with dreams and courage, strong within.

It's essential to record these moments. Whether it's in your journal, your phone or tablet, the back of your finished paper diary or the front of the new one, take some time and write up your thoughts and feelings. Note what you've done that you're proud of. Praise yourself for the qualities you've displayed. Record the people to whom you owe gratitude for their assistance, including those who have given you a tough time and made you learn the hard way. Take a minute to drop them a line and let them know how you feel. Nicely.

'....Praise yourself for the qualities you've displayed.'

Write up now where you will be in a year's time – and write it all in the present tense. Work out the three or four most important things in your life that you will give top commitment to for the year, and then work out how and when and where. Visualisation and affirmation, for instance, are well-known mind programmers. But possibly the most useful question for me is "If it's so important to you, why don't you have it already?

That's when you discover obstacles and roadblocks which need to be dealt with. Easy to program when you know what has to be done.

I had my speaker friend and colleague Daniel Johnson, now in Colorado, to thank for wonderful goal setting practices. He had some techniques that sort out your life and how you are spending it with a firm but gentle jolt. Thank you always, Daniel!

'....Be there. Do it....'

If you ask me for my formula for goal accomplishment, I'll give it to you in a few words; Be there. Do it.

For most of us, what we want is sitting there waiting to be taken. Little is beyond our reach. All it takes is the action step that makes it happen. It's true to say that successful people are the ones who do the things that unsuccessful people won't do. They just do it.

The rest of the world watches in wonder. Some of us read about it, some of us make time for seminars, webinars and podcasts, and find out how. All that's fantastic, and better than doing nothing. We are learning. growing in knowledge and confidence.

The winners, though, are the ones who go further, who take the action step that begins the journey.

I remember once sitting and feeling pretty miserable, self-indulgently sorry for myself, and unable to figure out what to do next. I remembered to ask my higher awareness, my voice of inner wisdom, how I could discover happiness. In an instant the voice answered "Just be happy'. I couldn't believe it. It was too easy. Surely there had to be more to it than that. But there wasn't.

Whatever you want to be, be it. Whatever you know is right for you to do, do it. And your goals are achieved. Some all at once, some a step at a time.

And you can do this on any day you choose, whatever the date on the calendar.

Today is New Year's Day. And so is tomorrow.

Your goals do not know what date it is. They only know whether you are committed to them or not. Whether you are doing everything you need to do to bring them into fruition.

They don't even know whether you have dark hair or blonde or none!

They don't know your age or your gender! And they don't know or care about your bank balance. So pull out your journal or start again in your diary (there's a lot of value in real old-fashioned handwriting, you know) and start dreaming, planning and committing to action.

Take the First Step, you First-Footer.

I'm special! You'd better believe it

"We can not build the future for our youth, but we can build our youth for the future...."

So spoke President Franklin Delano Roosevelt, at a time of economic crisis in America, in a period when success for anyone meant hanging on tightly to belief in oneself and not giving in, no matter what.

Life for us is not quite so tough. Most of our youth live in pretty comfortable surroundings, with shelter, food and clothing an assumed right, and a good education available for all. But still we worry, if not so much about their physical comforts and resources, a great deal about their mental and emotional strengths. Because although we have built a world where most physical desires can be readily gratified, we've learned in the process that mental and emotional stability does not come along with our comforts automatically - in fact they become even more elusive. It seems we are discovering that the wellbeing we always thought we could buy from the outside, means nothing unless we can find wellbeing on the inside.

And of course, like caring parents and teachers everywhere, we want to spare our young ones the same pain that we go through on our growth paths.

We can't. We can only prepare and equip them with the skills, beliefs and behaviours to deal with it.

How many of you, on listening to a self-discovery speaker, or reading a "how to improve your life" book, gasp with remembrance of years spent struggling unnecessarily, and wish that someone had told you a few real facts of life when you were still at school? Did anyone teach you goal setting? Time management? How to examine your own magnificent potential, and count up the great things you had already done, even at age 17? I don't know about you, but I and many of my friends recall that mediocrity was the prime objective - it was so important not to stand out, not to excel, above all else not to be special. At least at anything other than sport! It took me until my 20's to learn not to deny a compliment, to shake hands with a firm hand and a strong smile, to be proud of my uniqueness rather than try to bury it in conformity and embarrassment. Strange how we got far more embarrassed about being good than we did about being less than good!

> '....it was so important not to stand out, not to excel, above all else not to be special....'

Many people now work to ensure that our young people discover their magnificence and have the chance to look at their potential and believe in themselves, before they leave their high schools. One group I loved ran a great program for 15 and 16 year olds called "I'm Special". Designed by the indomitable Rita Hartney, my magnificent friend and mentor who has now passed, it was intended to be run in schools with the teachers present, usually over a six to eight week span with one hour per week. It was totally funded by donations and totally run by volunteers, both as organisers and as speakers. It had a powerful impact.

There was a mnemonic for I'M SPECIAL which you might find encouraging and inspirational for yourself – I do!

I is for Individuality - be yourself and proud of it!

M is for Management of Self - every one of us is responsible for our own actions, our own choices and the consequences of those choices.

S is for Sense of Direction - goals. As the Cheshire Cat says to Alice in Wonderland "if you don't know where you are going, then it really doesn't matter which road you take." And with no end destination in mind, you'll have no chance of getting there.

P is for Persistence - nothing in the world can take the place of it. Remember Winston Churchill's famous saying: Never, never, never, never give up! There are no failures in life, only failings. Making mistakes is a fabulous learning mechanism. Winning is coming fourth if you came fifth yesterday.

'....Winning is coming fourth if you came fifth yesterday...'

E is for Esteem - you can if you think you can. You are what you think you are - and you are special!

C is for Courage - to fight for what you know is right and to keep going in the face of the opposition.

I is for Image - you never get a second chance to make a first impression, and most people are hired (or not) in the first 30 seconds of a job interview. We need to understand the impact of dress and grooming, interview techniques, and even how to shake hands, when that is permitted.

A is for Attitude - it's really not the events in our lives that shape us, it's our attitude to those events. As W Clement Stone said, there is one thing over which each person has absolute, inherent control, and that is his or her own mental attitude.

L is for Love - not soppy sentimentality, but real active caring. Understanding that we all have a right to be ourselves, and that no one is here to live up to our expectations. Just allowing people to be - and helping them when they ask - that's love. And the first person deserving of our love is — our self.

Because we're special.

It's gratifying to see that the personal growth movement has encouraged so many people to believe in themselves.

But sometimes it seems that just as the self-esteem work is catching on, we're given another new set of higher standards to live up to. It must seem to many that no matter how hard they try, they can't reach the peak!

That's one of the reasons I'm so glad you're reading this book. Because you can help so many people to see that they have already reached the peak – at least the peak for today. The peak of today's possible. And none of us will ever reach the peak of perfection, because that's not possible.

All any of us can do is keep doing, keep learning growing and striving, and keep becoming more of the person we were born to be. Keep resting, relaxing, recovering, reviewing and reminding ourselves that every single one of us is different, and every one of us is inherently special. Because we were born that way.

This is dedicated to the memory of Margaret London, a State Director for the I'm Special Program who left us far too soon. She truly planted shade trees for others to shelter under.

It's about commitment

There's a famous saying of the great Ty Boyd's which is a particular favourite. "Commit yourself. Because until you do, you're just taking up space."

Pretty tough, isn't it? Very hard on some of the lovely, warm smiling people we come across all the time. Those who float gently through life without ever putting themselves on the line. Those who would never offend anyone and who don't take kindly to being asked to put up with such a firm demand on their existence. But there you are. Uncomfortably, the adage is true.

Commitment is a compulsory prerequisite to success in anything. Nobody ever got anywhere of value to them by just drifting there. 'Go with the flow' doesn't mean don't bother going at all.

An old Greek proverb says: "If a boat knows not to which port it is headed, no wind is favourable".

> '....Commitment is a compulsory prerequisite to success in anything...'

You've read of some of my challenges. So you know that I am not talking through the rose-coloured haze of an easy life.

I had a challenging childhood for all sorts of reasons, although loved and raised to the best of their ability by hard-working parents. Continual illness including asthma and polio, and several surgical operations before the age of 12. I was a clever student and artistic performer when that wasn't fashionable, and felt lonely and isolated most of the time.

On the surface? Bright, positive, even confident. One layer below? Terrified, unsure, lonely. No doubt many of you relate.

At 20 I left home and changed my country of residence. Alone. In hindsight, it was almost insane! But it worked. I grew – my career, my talents, my coping mechanisms, my friendships, and my sense of self.

The first major trauma came immediately after my marriage, to a glamorous handsome marketing manager in the travel industry. I was in bliss. Until one week after the wedding I tipped a packet of frozen French fries into a pan full of boiling oil - hit the handle in the shock of the explosion – and tossed the entire contents all over my face, neck, hands and naked upper torso.

Several months and graft surgery later, I was home and healing, thrilled to discover an unexpected pregnancy and ultimately the birth of my beautiful son. He was, and is still, the gift of my life.

But not long after his birth his father lost his job. We lived on savings for a while, but eventually I had to wean my three month old baby, leave him in day care and return to work full time. Now that is fairly commonplace. Then, unprepared emotionally and socially, it was extremely challenging, physically and mentally.

Within two years, with both of us in management roles, I had hired a lovely young woman to tend my little boy by day. Unfortunately she also tended my husband, and our marriage was over.

The grief was deep, suppressed as a coping mechanism beneath a veneer of strength and capability. But, as many of you will know, that need to care for someone else simply takes over and carries us through.

And eventually, when the time is right, we must rest and recover.

My friend Marilynn Semonick sent me this prayer recently; I believe it is a Franciscan Benediction, and it speaks to me of our journey through the pain of life towards the success we seek:

> *May God bless you with discomfort...*
> *Discomfort at easy answers, half-truths and superficial relationships,*
> *Discomfort, so that you will live deep within your heart.*
>
> *May God bless you with anger...*
> *Anger at injustice, oppression, and exploitation of people,*
> *Anger, so that you will work for justice, freedom, and peace.*
>
> *May God bless you with tears...*
> *Tears to shed for those who suffer pain, rejection, starvation and war,*
> *Tears, so that you will reach out to comfort them*
> *And turn their pain into joy.*
>
> *And, may God bless you with foolishness...*
> *Foolishness to believe that you can make a difference in this world,*
> *Foolishness, so that you will do what others claim cannot be done.*

I learned back then, and I have learned several times since, that full-blown commitment will sweep away every obstacle. I have seen it happen in my own life again and again, and if you reflect

'.....full-blown commitment will sweep away every obstacle.'

153

on all the success stories you know, you will recognise the same thing. I have observed that the whole world stands aside for the one who knows where he or she is going. And all becomes possible.

Commitment is an uncomfortable word from some people. "Promises were meant to be broken" has almost become an acceptable adage in some circles. It seems so sad that all those old stories of a "person's word is their bond" no longer seem so vital a part of our children's upbringing.

The defence of a person's honour, his or her commitment to perceived responsibilities and obligations, used to be a principal guiding rule for conduct. For some notable, noticeable people it still is. Take a look at those people, and see if they are achieving their objectives in life. Because if they are, their commitment is the key.

Some years of my business experience were spent in an organisation which used a particular system for identifying people with the best sales potential.

One of the essential characteristics for success was ethics. The person with ethics was not defined as the one who did not lie, cheat or steal, but rather the one who always did what he or she said they would do. That's commitment. The people who keep promises - and know that the ones they make to themselves are the most important of all.

Unfortunately in many of our major corporations, progress - both individual and corporate - can be impeded by politics or power games. It can become very difficult for a salesperson or executive in his or her career to declare a particular stance, or display a point of view, if it does not match the prevailing leader's.

Game playing can be the normal code of existence, jockeying for position, trying to get approval, pretending to be who or what you are not in order to get support. Horrible! Ghastly! Even pathetic! It is time-wasting, unnecessary, in many cases dishonest, and often self-defeating. Please take a stand against it. If you don't stand for something you'll fall for anything.

Take a stand and declare it. Support it, and defend it. If you learn you are wrong, amend it. But the person who sits on the fence usually ends up being fairly uncomfortable.

My very favourite words on commitment come from a quote from WH Murray, the leader of the Scottish Himalayan Expedition in 1951, which refers to the philosopher Goethe. They were first given to me by an art teacher - I was amazed then at their truth and have rediscovered it several times even lately.

"Until one is committed, there is hesitancy, the chance to draw back, always ineffectiveness.

"Concerning all acts of initiative (and creation), there is one elementary truth, the ignorance of which kills countless ideas and splendid plans.

"That the moment one definitely commits oneself, then Providence moves too.

'All sorts of things occur to help one that would never otherwise have occurred. A whole stream of events issues from the decision, raising in one's favour all manner of unforeseen incidents and meetings and material assistance, which no man could have dreamed would have come his way. I learned a deep respect for one of Goethe's couplets:

"Whatever you can do, or dream you can, begin it.

Boldness has Genius, Power and Magic in it.

Begin it now."

Yes please. That's the pathway to Success.

I wrote the following Message once for a conference of educators, and I've continually been asked for reprints ever since. So here it is for you:

A Message for You...

Please remember that no-one in the history of the human race
has made, or can make, the contribution that you can.
You are uniquely valuable. You can not be compared to another.
You can never be as good as they are, and they can never be as good as you.
Your unique gifts and abilities are precious, and their value is unquestionable.

It is your responsibility to make the most of them and to use them
to be of service.
That is your only challenge.

Catherine Palin-Brinkworth

Thank you for sharing a part of your life with us. If we can help you to reach your success in any way, please be in contact.

Progress Performance International

P O Box 1397
Surfers Paradise Q 4217
Australia

P O Box 710
Broadway NSW 2007
Australia

manager@progressperformance.com

Printed in the United States
By Bookmasters